CHANGING PARENTAL ATTITUDES THROUGH GROUP DISCUSSION

THE HOGG FOUNDATION RESEARCH SERIES

WAYNE H. HOLTZMAN, Editor

Tornadoes over Texas . . . . by HARRY ESTILL MOORE
Electrical Stimulation of the Brain . . edited by DANIEL E. SHEER
Inkblot Perception and Personality . . . WAYNE H. HOLTZMAN, JOSEPH S. THORPE, JON D. SWARTZ and E. WAYNE HERRON

Changing Parental Attitudes through Group Discussion

CARL F. HEREFORD

Published for the HOGG FOUNDATION FOR MENTAL HEALTH

by the UNIVERSITY OF TEXAS PRESS, AUSTIN

Library of Congress Catalog Card No. 63–11192

Manufactured in the United States of America

Foreword

A CONSIDERABLE AMOUNT HAS BEEN WRITTEN ABOUT EDUcating parents through the group-discussion method, but the number of well-designed, objective studies evaluating the effectiveness of this method for changing parental attitudes and behavior is exceedingly small. Indeed, one might almost say practically nonexistent. It is a most difficult feat to maintain the experimental controls necessary for rigorous evaluation of the method when working with volunteers from community organizations and with parents who are completely free to choose whether or not they wish to participate in such research. Implementing a community research plan is a quite different matter from designing it to meet scientific standards in the first place.

The outstanding success of the Austin, Texas, community-education project in parent-child relations can be attributed chiefly to the patient, gentle but resolute manner in which Carl Hereford and his colleagues involved members of the community in every stage of their project from the very start. Under the facilitating influence of the Hogg Foundation, the preliminary phases of the project were carefully worked through by representatives of the Austin-Travis County Mental Health Society, the Austin Congress of Parents and Teachers, the public schools, and relevant departments in the University of Texas. During the four-year period of the research project, more than a hundred nonprofessional men and women completed special courses designed to train them to lead group discussions, and many hundreds of parents participated in the educational phase of the project. That the program of parent education by the discussion method continues to thrive in Austin long after the research project itself has been terminated testifies to the enthusiasm with which it has been received throughout the community.

The accomplishments set forth in this book, the fourth monograph in the Foundation's Research Series published by the University of Texas Press, come closest to fulfilling the Foundation's goal of major emphasis upon action research dealing with significant community mental health problems, for the educational method investigated here can be applied in a wide variety of community settings with a minimum of outside professional assistance. Moreover, the need to discover a feasible method for improving parent-child relations on a large scale is particularly significant for an age in which so much depends upon realizing fully our potentials for development as mature individuals. That Dr. Hereford's findings clearly point to the superiority of group discussions, moderated by trained nonprofessional leaders, for improving parental attitudes and behavior and the behavior of the children of these parents serves to dramatize the importance of a greatly increased effort devoted to developing similar educational programs in other communities.

To speak clearly and meaningfully to two very different kinds of readers is not easy to accomplish within a single text. It is to the author's credit that he has made a sustained attempt to achieve this complex aim in the present book. In the first five chapters he discusses chiefly the major purposes of the program, the nature of the discussion method employed, and the practical problems one would likely encounter in setting up a program of this kind in any community. This portion should be particularly helpful to the educator, community worker, or parents' organization contemplating a similar program, while at the same time providing valuable background information for the specialist primarily interested in the research design and outcome.

The major portion of the book, however, is devoted to the research evaluating the educational program. The psychologist, sociologist, and educational-research specialist will find here sufficient documentation of the research design, procedures, and analysis to judge for himself the worth of the undertaking and the relative merits of the several educational techniques evaluated. Doubtless the general reader, too, will find most of this material interesting and meaningful.

Three shorter publications, designed for groups wishing to use the discussion method with nonprofessional leaders, have already appeared under the auspices of the Foundation. *Leading Group Discussions*, by Frank Cheavens, director of Community Education for the Austin project, has already gone into its fourth printing as a training handbook for discussion leaders. *Organizing Group Discussions*, by Carl Hereford, is a straightforward account of how to develop a program utilizing group discussion. *Developing Discussion Leaders in Brief Workshops*, also by Dr. Cheavens, tells how to conduct the leadership training courses which prepare individuals to lead group discussions. The present book, the final volume in the series based on the Austin project, provides the theoretical and empirical basis for the discussion method as outlined in these popularly written pamphlets. Together they form an effective set of materials for practitioner and research specialist alike.

WAYNE H. HOLTZMAN
Associate Director
Hogg Foundation for Mental Health

Preface

On July 4, 1955, a group of citizens professionally trained in mental health met in Austin, Texas, to discuss ways of improving mental health education in their city. The Project described in this book was the outgrowth of that meeting. The willingness of these busy people to give up a holiday to discuss this endeavor set the tone that carried throughout the entire Project; without the volunteer help of these and many other public-spirited men and women the realization of this undertaking would not have been possible. The same concern for the civic welfare was shown by the paid staff also, many of whom went far beyond their normal duties to make the Project a success.

This original group of professionals, with some additions, became the Research Council of the Project, and provided valuable guidance, policy formation, and technical consultation. The educational program of the Project was sponsored in the community by the Mental Health Association of Austin-Travis County, largely through the efforts of Charles H. Dent and Mrs. Eleanor Eisenberg, who later also trained discussion leaders and organized group discussions. The Austin Community Guidance Center sponsored the research activities, and was the agency that received funds granted the Project. Thanks are due William C. Adamson, and John A. Boston, Jr., directors of the Center, for their interest in the Project. The financial support came from grants by the Hogg Foundation for Mental Health of the University of Texas, and the National Institute of Mental Health.

The work of the Project was greatly facilitated by the loyalty and interest of a hard-working staff. Credit goes to Frank Cheavens for organizing the training program for nonprofessional leaders, and to Edward C. Moseley for doing much of the statistical analysis, including many all-night sessions operating the computer. Special thanks are due Mrs. Charles Cleland, Mrs. Jim Eichelberger, and Mrs. W. W. Hunt, who not only performed their regular secretarial duties but did yeoman service as research assistants, statistical clerks, public-relations representatives—in short, in whatever came to hand. The interviewers for the Project performed services far beyond what could be expected for the small remuneration they received, tracking down parents, keeping night appointments, and making up broken appointments.

I wish to thank Irby Carruth, superintendent of the Austin Public Schools, for permission to carry out our program in the school system. My thanks also go to the principals and teachers who assisted us, many times with enthusiasm and interest. The educational program actually reached the parents through the elementary-school PTA's. Sincere thanks are given to the many PTA officers and committee chairmen who spent hours making arrangements for the discussion groups.

The nonprofessional leaders contributed hundreds of hours of voluntary community service under the auspices of the Project. Theirs is a record of outstanding achievement in responsible citizenship. Not once in four years did a leader fail to meet his group. The observers, many of whom were neophyte leaders, must also be credited for performing a tedious and thankless task, also on an unpaid basis.

The hundreds of Austin parents who took time from their busy schedules to be interviewed deserve much praise. They received no reward and were not even aware of the aims of the Project; their time was purely a contribution to research.

The manuscript was critically reviewed by Robert L. Sutherland, Mrs. Bert K. Smith, and Harold Stevenson. They have my thanks for many helpful suggestions. The final form of the manuscript was typed by Mrs. Pearl S. Gardner.

My principal debt of gratitude is owed to Wayne H. Holtzman. His interest and help were a major factor in the success of this undertaking. He provided continuing stimulation, support, and technical assistance throughout the entire course of the Project, and his assistance with the manuscript was invaluable.

Finally, I thank my wife, Evelyn, not only for her encouragement and forbearance but also for serving as a sounding board and collaborator throughout the Project and during the preparation of the manuscript.

CFH

Austin, Texas

Contents

Figures

Tables

CHANGING PARENTAL ATTITUDES THROUGH GROUP DISCUSSION

I

Educating the Parent for Parenthood

A TREMENDOUS AMOUNT OF TIME AND MONEY IS BEING spent in the United States in an effort to help parents become more effective in their parental roles. One has only to open the pages of any magazine whose special appeal is to women or to attend a PTA meeting to realize that the emphasis on this subject is on the increase. Nor is this emphasis on educating adults limited to parent-child relations; it is also taking place in such other areas of mental health as marital relationships and personal adjustment. People are interested in learning how to establish better human relations, and how to attain a fuller and happier way of life.

At present the mass media carry the bulk of the effort to inform parents on child-rearing practices. Very few parents actually attend courses on parenthood offered in a regular educational program. Various organizations reach many parents through programs on parent-child relations, frequently consisting of a lecture by an expert, or a panel discussion, or perhaps a film, but these are usually sporadic attempts, with no continuity intended. The choice of content is dependent upon the convenience of the speaker rather than upon its appropriateness to an over-all program. Some material regarding parent-child relations is presented on radio and television, but such incidental programs seldom constitute formal educational attempts; concepts of parenthood and child rearing are likely to be expressed indirectly rather than as the specific object of the program. But by far the major portion of parent information is offered through magazine articles and pamphlets. An issue of a woman's magazine without at least one article on parenthood or child-rearing practices is almost a rarity, and even the periodicals which reach wider audiences are finding that this type of article has high reader-interest. Most of these articles, however, written by journalists who naturally cannot be specialists in all fields, suffer from faults of interpretation as well as oversimplification. Pamphlets, on the other hand, usually are written by professionals and are distributed through some organization that has the promoting of education as one of its functions or goals.

Unlike some other areas of education, that of parent-child relations is concerned primarily not with knowledge, information, and facts, but with concepts, ideas, and attitudes. Since the ultimate goal in any attempt at educating parents in the parental role is to change the parent's behavior in his relations with his child, merely providing the parent with factual information and knowledge is not enough. The parent who has "read all the books and pamphlets," who can talk the jargon, who *knows* all about parent-child relations and yet is unhappy and ineffective with his own children, is all too familiar a sight. It is also quite common to see a parent who has had little instruction about child-rearing practices and no inclination for more who does a superior job of bringing up his children. The main educational problem in parent-child relations, then, may be viewed as not one of giving information or imparting knowledge. The main problem lies in those parental difficulties which stem not from ignorance but from attitudes, feelings, and emotions.

From this point of view, therefore, the most appropriate goal of an educational program for parents is that of attitudinal change, which will, in turn, lead to behavioral change. Given this as the object, the content of the educational program assumes much less importance; the focus of interest is placed on the method itself. This de-emphasis of content also makes sense in view of the fact that there is no well-established and generally accepted body of factual knowledge regarding parent-child relations. It would, indeed, be difficult to find very many areas of complete agreement among the experts in the field of parent-child relations, and even the small amount of agreement that does exist seems to vary from time to time. The theory of rigid feeding schedules for infants in the nineteen-twenties, for example, gave way to permissiveness in the forties; and undoubtedly some other approach will be advocated with equal certainty in the future. The fact of the matter is that the parent-child relation, like any other human relation, tends to be complex and personal, and what is effective in one situation will not be effective in another. It is because of this uniqueness that experts are so reluctant to give advice, prescriptions, or, many times, even specific information, to large groups or through mass media. Learning about parent-child relations is not the same as learning the facts of electronics or biology. Unfortunately, in parent-child relations there is no body of factual information having universal applicability.

If the emphasis in an educational program for parents is to be not on content but on attitudinal change, then the problem of values arises. Which attitudes are good and which are not? If there is no general agreement on the body of factual information for achieving desirable parent-child relations, is there any better agreement on which attitudes should be considered desirable?

The basic philosophy that underlies the educational approach presented in this book is that of individual growth and self-development. Accordingly, it is not here proposed that parents should be educated in the "correct" way to bring up children. They are not to be told "how to do it." They are not to be provided with a blueprint for happy family living. Instead, the educational program presented here is directed at helping the individual parent to grow in his own way, the way that is appropriate for him and for his relations with his child. It offers him the opportunity to develop his potentials, to find for himself the attitudes, values, and modes of behavior that are most effective and rewarding in his own parent-child relations. It holds that the basic responsibility for growth and change lies within the individual parent, not in the educator. There is no "organization man" among the ranks of parents, no pattern of behavior that is "right," no set of attitudes or feelings that are universally appropriate. There is only, in the last analysis, the individual with his own potentials and limitations, his uniqueness, and his basic capacity to grow and develop as a parent.

If the goal of parental education is viewed as the changing of attitudes and behavior and not the mere imparting of information, then the various techniques or methods of education should be examined in light of this. It seems probable that a well-written, interesting, and accurate pamphlet might do a reasonably good job of transmitting factual information. It is doubtful, however, that such a pamphlet would result in any substantial change of attitude on the part of its reader. Herein lies the basic weakness of mass media as a means of educating parents. Although the mass media do provide a cheap and efficient means of reaching a large number of people, these recipients remain essentially passive. They read the pamphlet, look at the film, or listen to the program, but they do not participate; and while informational learning is possible without participation, attitudinal change is not. Parents may read an article or pamphlet, but when they have finished, their attitudes and their actual behavior are very likely to remain unchanged.[1]

If the mass media make their appeal largely to the intellectual rather than to the emotional aspects of learning, and if their role is primarily that of giving information, then what type of program for parents can achieve attitudinal learning and change? If participation by the learner is to be a part of our educational method, we immediately face serious questions as to expense and feasibility. For example, might the ideal solution be individual psychotherapy for each parent—a psychotherapy designed not to "cure" or solve problems, but to enhance and further personal growth and development? Such a goal is, of course, completely unrealistic. There are not enough mental health professionals to take care of the clinical needs of our population, much less the educational needs. An educational program based on the use of experts, then, either through lectures, classes, or workshops, cannot reach a substantial segment of the population because of the shortage of such experts. Furthermore, this shortage shows no promise of improving. Our recruitment and training in the mental health profession are not keeping pace with the increase in the general population.[2]

Expense and lack of trained personnel are not the only drawbacks to those educational methods which are based on the use of experts. While the expert is, of course, a more personal factor than the mass media, and while there is an opportunity for participation through asking questions and interacting with the expert, the passivity of the recipient, in an emotional sense, is still there. It is the expert who knows the answers, who gives the advice, who takes the responsibility for the content of the educational program, not the learner. In this age of the expert and the special-

[1] See L. W. Rowland, *A First Evaluation of the "Pierre the Pelican" Mental Health Pamphlets*, Louisiana Mental Health Studies No. 1 (New Orleans, Louisiana Society for Mental Health, 1948).

[2] G. W. Albee, *Mental Health Manpower Trends* (New York, Basic Books, 1959).

ist, our tendency is to turn to the expert and let him solve our problem for us. This is frequently a very sound approach; we live in a complex world and no man has the knowledge, training, and skill to deal with all its complexities. But there are certain areas of life that cannot be turned over to the expert, areas in which we must, for better or worse, "do it ourselves." Becoming educated is one of these areas. Paying the tuition at a good school does not insure the acquisition of knowledge. The finest teacher in the world cannot teach a child who will not learn. This is particularly true of attitudinal learning and changing behavior. We cannot ask the expert, no matter how wise he is, what our attitudes should be on some particular topic, and then adopt that attitude, for attitudes are based not only on intellect but also on emotions, and must therefore be changed or modified through our own efforts and experiences. When we turn to the expert we are likely to relinquish our own personal involvement and effort in order to profit from his knowledge and experience.

There are other frequently voiced criticisms of the traditional methods of parent education. For example, both the mass-media method and expert-based method tend to reach the middle classes primarily, and hence are particularly ineffective in lower-class cultures. Indeed, it appears that much of the educational material is directed at the middle classes, in method and in content. Here again is a rather obvious disadvantage of relying upon the mass media as instruments of education. The materials can be presented in only one way; they cannot be altered or rephrased for each possible recipient. The same is true, in general, of the lecturer for the expert-based method. He obviously cannot "speak the language" of everyone at the same time.

Why, then, in spite of these inherent and seemingly basic difficulties in helping parents to do a better job of child rearing, have activities in this area continued to flourish? The answer lies in the demand. When demand is strong enough, something will usually arise to meet it. The effectiveness of programs for parents is often judged on the basis of popular demand rather than improved interpersonal relations or child-rearing practices. A magazine publisher considers an article on these subjects a success if it sells many copies of his magazine. If there is a big demand for a pamphlet on parent-child relations, then it, too, is considered successful. Similarly, if a lecturer can attract a large audience for a talk on discipline, then the program is considered successful. The truth of the matter is, however, that very little is known about the real effectiveness of most attempts at parent education. We may know how many people came to the lecture or how many people bought the pamphlet, but we do not know what effect these methods had in changing attitudes and behavior. In relation to the time and money spent by educators and learners as well, the amount of evaluative research is practically negligible; and the quality of even this small amount tends, with a few exceptions, to be crude and superficial.[3]

The prospective evaluator of education immediately finds himself faced with the almost insurmountable difficulty of his complete inability to control variables, and the most frequent result of this difficulty is that he must rely on the evaluation given by the recipient of the education. The use of an evaluative questionnaire can give some indication of whether or not the recipient liked the program, but it reveals very little about its effectiveness in achieving the goal of attitudinal change.

Nevertheless, the difficulties inherent in evaluative research on educational efforts by no means diminish the necessity of such research. The enormous amount of time, money, and effort already invested in helping parents to do a better job has clearly substantiated the need for research that can assess with validity the effectiveness of what is being done. The development of an educational program in mental health is only half the job—the other half is to determine its effectiveness. In making this determination the criteria of acceptance by the public and the popularity of the program are not sufficient. Evaluation of education in parent-child relations must concern itself first with attitude change and ultimately with behavior change.

The Research Project described in this book represents an attempt to accomplish two aims: first, to develop and establish in a community a workable method of helping parents with their parent-child relations; second, to evaluate this method in terms of the resulting attitudinal and behavioral changes.

The four-year study was conducted in selected elementary schools in Austin, Texas, over the years 1955–1960. All the subjects were residents of Austin except fifty-six parents from Taylor, Texas, who formed part of the standardization group for one of the measuring instruments.

[3] National Institute of Mental Health, *Evaluation in Mental Health*, Public Health Service Publication No. 413 (Washington, U.S. Government Printing Office, 1955).

II

The Discussion-Group Method

IF THE GOAL OF PARENTAL EDUCATION IS SELF-DEVELOPment through attitudinal change, then a method for achieving this purpose must meet several criteria.

CRITERIA FOR AN EFFECTIVE EDUCATIONAL PROGRAM

1. The method must provide for participation by the parent. For attitudinal change to take place, the learner cannot be passive; he must become actively involved in the educational process.

2. The method must be feasible; that is, the program must be realistic and practicable within the reasonable limitations of our typical society. Psychotherapy for all might or might not be a desirable goal, but universal psychotherapy is such a completely unrealistic concept that the question of its desirability is inconsequential. In effect, this second criterion almost precludes the use of professionals in direct educational activities, for there are not now, nor will there be in the foreseeable future, enough professionals to meet the need.

3. The method must be economical. While it is true that a great deal of time and money is being spent to help parents, it is also true that there are a great many parents, and in order to reach a substantial number of them and still remain within the bounds of economic reality the unit cost per parent will have to be relatively low. This means that, in so far as possible, the method not only must use existing facilities and work

through presently operating organizations but also it must make every effort to utilize volunteer help fully. It also means that the program should get results in a relatively brief period, for the longer the time, the greater the cost.

4. The method must be acceptable and interesting to parents. It makes little difference how good the program is if parents do not attend. This acceptance and interest must extend up and down the social-class range, with particular attention given to the lower classes, where educational methods so often fail. It seems reasonable to assume that at least a substantial number of parents have the motivation to learn more about themselves in their parental role, but the mere existence of this motivation is not enough to insure their attendance at the program.

5. The method must be testable by evaluative research so that its effectiveness can be determined.

The method which seems to meet these standards best is that of the discussion group, primarily because it affords a maximum of participation and personal involvement, as stipulated in the first criterion, but also because it can be modified and organized in such a way as to satisfy the other criteria.

The discussion technique itself is probably as old as civilized man. Indeed, our democratic tradition itself is based in part on discussion, on the idea of talking things over together, on the concept of everyone's being able to have his say. The use of discussion in political and governmental institutions is well established as a system for solving problems. The use of discussion techniques as an educational means, however, is a more recent development, and the history of education contains much more of didactic methodology than it does of discussion techniques.

Two essential elements are involved in the discussion method of education. The first is that of participation, for in all areas we learn by doing. The concept of having the student take part in the educational process has become firmly entrenched in our teaching procedures, regardless of the content of the particular program. The second point—not quite so obvious as the first, nor so generally applicable where content is concerned—is personal involvement on the part of the learner. In the course of participation the individual invests some of himself in the educational procedure. He becomes ego-involved and uses not only his intellect but his emotions as well. This kind of personal involvement may not be essential to intellectual or academic learning, or to learning in content areas that have no high emotional loading for the learner. In areas that do involve emotions, attitudes, and feelings, however—that is, areas with a high affective component—personal involvement appears to be essential. The force of one's reason is usually weakened by attitudes, prejudices, and feelings, for they are rooted not in logic but in emotions. Change in these areas, therefore, calls for an educational experience which has a high degree of personal involvement.

DEVELOPMENT OF THE TECHNIQUES

The use of group-discussion techniques for the purpose of parent education on a large scale was undertaken in 1950 by the St. Louis Mental Health Association under the leadership of Dr. Margaret Gildea.[1] The St. Louis program was centered around the nonprofessional discussion leader or, to use the pertinent terminology, the "lay" leader. This program later became a part of a much larger one designed to meet the mental health needs of the community not only at an educational but at a therapeutic level as well.[2]

In St. Louis, the discussion program was used primarily as one of the regular monthly presentations of an elementary-school PTA: that is, a film on parent-child relations and a group discussion presided over by the discussion leader took the place of one of the monthly programs arranged through the PTA. While this approach proved highly successful, and demonstrated quite clearly that large groups could and would respond to a nonprofessional discussion leader, the effectiveness of the group-discussion technique seemed to be minimized in several respects. Of first importance, perhaps, was the fact that it was a "one-shot" program. Although this one monthly meeting was devoted to the discussion of parent-child relations, all the rest of the meetings throughout the year

[1] Ellen L. Brashear, Eleanor T. Kenney, A. D. Buchmueller, and Margaret C.-L. Gildea, "A Community Program of Mental Health Education Using Group Discussion Methods," *American Journal of Orthopsychiatry*, Vol. 24 (1954), p. 554; and Margaret C.-L. Gildea, *Community Mental Health* (Springfield, Illinois, Charles C Thomas, 1959). For a popular account of the program, see Margaret Hickey, "A Community Promotes Mental Health," *Ladies Home Journal* (April, 1954), p. 29.

[2] J. C. Glidewell, *An Evaluation of a Preventive Community Mental Health Program*, Progress Report IV (Clayton, Missouri, St. Louis County Health Department, 1960). Mimeograph.

were devoted to typical PTA affairs (a talk on school safety, a concert, the activities of the Scout troop). Therefore, in spite of the fact that the PTA members did participate in the discussion when the program was on parent-child relations, it seemed unlikely that a single exposure to the subject during the school year would result in any extensive or lasting change in basic attitudes or behavior. Furthermore, the groups at the PTA meetings were too large for effective discussions. The size of the group, plus the time limitations (one hour allotted for the program, including the twenty to thirty minutes taken up by the film), made it impossible for everyone in the group to have a chance to participate. Finally, and importantly, the participant was not committed to even the topic of parent-child relations, much less to the discussion method itself. The PTA members probably came to the regular monthly meeting without having given much thought to the nature of the discussion that would take place or to its ramifications.

These three factors appear to place severe limitations on the effectiveness of this use of the discussion method in changing parental attitudes and in providing for parents' growth and self-development. It is interesting that, despite these inhibitory factors, the program has been successful in St. Louis to the extent that this kind of discussion group with a nonprofessional leader has been very much in demand.

The Project under evaluation in this book was based on the St. Louis Mental Health Association's Program, but with modifications designed to correct the undesirable factors already discussed. The use of nonprofessional leaders and the method for training them were taken over almost directly from the St. Louis plan. The actual execution of the program, however, was substantially modified. In our revised program the discussion-group method was not used as a regular program of the PTA's monthly meeting, but was organized as a separate series of meetings under the sponsorship of the PTA, although not limited to its members. All parents in the elementary-school district were invited to attend a series of six weekly discussion meetings. This plan had two principal advantages: PTA membership was not essential; and, most important, the full series of six meetings would provide the parents with adequate exposure to this method of education. Furthermore, the size of the group was controlled, for it was planned to have the group limited to about fifteen members. When the number of people interested in attending the meetings exceeded the total that could be successfully handled in one group, then a second, or even a third group, was set up. In the single instance in which an elementary-school district yielded too few people for a discussion group of the proper size, we combined this group with another. Since the sole purpose of the meetings was to discuss parent-child relations, the entire two-hour period was used for this purpose. Nothing else was scheduled on the program—no business meeting, no announcements, none of the busywork that usually takes up the time of an organization. The increase in the number of meetings, the increase in the time allotted for these meetings, and the limitation on the number of parents in each group greatly increased the amount of participation possible for each parent.

Our final modifications were the use of explanatory publicity regarding the meetings and a system of registration for the participants. The parents in a given elementary-school district were informed of the topic (parent-child relations), of the method (group discussion), and even of the nonprofessional aspect of the leadership. They were then given an opportunity to register for the discussion-group series by returning a post card, though it was, of course, entirely possible to attend the meetings without sending in the card. This advance knowledge of both the nature of the meetings and the registration process itself was designed to produce in the participants a sort of commitment to the educational program. As a result, the discussion group was not a casual experience for parents who chanced upon it by simply attending the regular monthly meeting of their PTA; it was a clearly defined educational program in parent-child relations for parents who were interested in attending such a program.

III

The Nonprofessional Leader

It might seem that there could be nothing new or unique about setting up a series of meetings for group education. Study groups are quite common in many fields and are used by many different types of organizations. Even the use of the discussion technique in study groups is not unfamiliar to adult education, and although most adult groups are set up on some other educational basis, the use of discussion is becoming more and more frequent. The unusual aspect of this program, however, is the role of the nonprofessional discussion leader.

BASIC FUNCTION AND PERSONAL QUALITIES OF THE LEADER

The use of nonprofessionals as discussion leaders has been touched upon in the preceding chapters in relation to the critical shortage of professionals and to the economic advantages of volunteer help. But feasibility and economy were not the primary considerations in our use of nonprofessionals. Since the twin goals of the educational program of the Project were attitudinal change and personal growth and development, it was necessary not only to maximize the participation of the individual parent, but also to maximize his personal involvement with the educational process. The main problem was the need *to place on the participants rather than on the leader the responsibility for the program.*

The professional or expert is, of course, seriously hampered when he attempts to shift responsibility to his audience. He can give information, he can answer questions, he can even lead discussions, but basically the responsibility for the educational program is his and in almost every instance will continue to be his as long as he is present. Ours is an expert-oriented culture, and when the expert is present the responsibility for what takes place is almost axiomatically his, whether he desires it or not. As noted earlier, in many educational settings this situation is not undesirable. Indeed, in certain kinds of learning it is essential. But when emotional growth and development are the goal of a program, the inability of the expert to shift the basic responsibility for the program to the group members themselves makes his presence an inhibitory influence.

The nonprofessional leader does not work under this handicap. He literally cannot take the basic responsibility for guiding and directing the group because he is no more an expert in the subject under discussion than any other member of the group. He has been trained to use his skill mainly in moderating the discussion, not in directing it. He provides no content, gives no advice, solves no problems, but serves instead in the facilitating capacity of helping the members of the group understand and achieve their own purposes and goals. Hence responsibility for the program falls on the group itself and thereby on each individual member. With this responsibility come the ego-involvement and participation on an emotional level that make possible attitudinal change. The group member is not exhorted or taught. What is accomplished in the group is brought about solely through the efforts of each individual. Since the group belongs to the participant (not to an expert, not to a chairman), what is brought out in the course of discussion is therefore much more likely to influence the group member's attitude and emotion instead of merely adding to his knowledge and information.

The basic requirement for discussion leadership of this type is an outgoing nature, characterized primarily by a genuine interest in other people and sensitivity toward them. Usually a competent group-discussion leader will have demonstrated his capacity for leadership previously in some manner. He is likely to be active and busy. As would be expected, he must have a liking for others and fairly strong needs to serve and help them. Although the first prerequisite of a leader seems to be an outgoing personality (the introvert has too much difficulty in handling the multiple interpersonal relations present in a group), he cannot be the dominant, overbearing, aggressive type of individual that is frequently seen as a committee chairman or an officer in many organizations. He needs real sensitivity so far as interpersonal relations are concerned, as well as a high degree of flexibility and acceptance of others. Accordingly, a good leader must be essentially nonjudgmental. That is, he must not devalue a contribution by a group member even though it is divergent from his own attitude or opinion, and this attitude of acceptance must be real; it cannot be mere lip service. This attitude requires a firm conviction that everyone has something worthwhile to offer, and a genuine belief in each individual's capacity to grow and develop in the way that is most meaningful for him as an individual.

The nonprofessional leader cannot have any personal axes to grind or any point of view that he wishes to convey. He must unequivocally accept the fact that his job—his only job—is to facilitate the processes of the group, and not to guide or direct the members to a certain position or point of view. The measure of effectiveness of a leader is in direct proportion to his willingness to allow the group to assume full responsibility. Paradoxically, a good discussion leader does not have to be a person accustomed to public speaking or even one who always feels at ease before large groups. The atmosphere of group discussion is informal and intimate, and the leader's status is more nearly that of group membership than it is of group leadership. Many prospective leaders who have expressed a great deal of doubt about their competence to "lead" a group have later felt quite comfortable in moderating group discussions. One of the sources of anxiety for the prospective nonprofessional leader is the fear that he will be unable to answer the questions or provide the content for the discussion. As soon as he understands that this is not his role or responsibility, he becomes much more confident in the role of moderator.

A large part of the nonprofessional leader's strength lies in the fact that he is not an expert in matters that a group will discuss. It does not follow, however, that he needs neither skill nor training or that everyone can lead this kind of discussion group. An effective leader must have certain personality characteristics and develop certain skills. His characteristics and skills are not necessarily those typical of the expert; indeed, it seems that the professional's training and experience, many times, work against him so far as being a good discussion leader is concerned.

It is, of course, possible for an expert to be a good leader, but it is not inevitable. Conversely, neither can it be assumed that because an individual is not an expert, he is capable of being a good discussion leader. Since moderating a discussion group does require training and skill, a series of workshops directed by professionals was organized to select and train citizens from the community to serve as leaders.

SELECTION, TRAINING, AND ROLE OF THE LEADER

Six workshops were held during a period of four years to train nonprofessional leaders to moderate the discussion-group series for the Project. Of the 235 people who attended at least one meeting of the workshops, 104 of them finished the training. While almost all the leaders who completed the training later assumed some form of discussion leadership in the community, the Project itself utilized 22 of them. Since accepting the role of discussion leader is purely voluntary, it was necessary to keep a fairly sizable pool of trained and experienced leaders available in order to meet the demands of our program.

We tried several methods of recruiting prospective leaders. For the first workshop, prospects who either were known personally to the Project staff or who had been recommended to it were individually approached. While this system was satisfactory for obtaining a sufficient number of trainees for the first workshop, it became apparent that many qualified and interested people were being overlooked. For this reason, prospects for subsequent workshops were recruited principally by fairly widespread publicity directed toward people who were neither known to the Project staff nor recommended to it. For example, invitations were issued to all officers and committee chairmen of the elementary-school PTA's. Although the proportion of those recruited was relatively small compared to the number solicited, the method did secure adequate numbers of trainees for the workshops and enabled us to locate a substantial number of excellent prospects. Two other sources of prospects emerged as the Project progressed. Trained leaders frequently suggested persons who they thought would make good leaders, and these recommendations were nearly always sound. Moreover, as the various discussion-group series got underway, leaders would occasionally recommend that participants in their groups be trained as leaders. These recommendations also resulted usually in a good trainee.

The only serious difficulty in recruiting leaders was with the two ethnic minorities in the community. To insure maximum participation in the discussion groups, we felt it desirable to have Negro leaders for the Negro groups and Latin-American leaders for the groups of parents whose children attended schools in which the population was predominantly Latin American. Through contacts made by Negro members of the Mental Health Association, enough prospects were obtained to insure an adequate number of Negro leaders. Since efforts to persuade prospective Latin-American leaders to attend the regular workshops failed consistently, it was decided to hold a workshop specifically for them. This proved to be one of the most difficult undertakings of the entire Project. It was soon discovered that the term "parent-child relations" simply does not hold the same attraction for the Latin-American subculture that it does for middle-class Anglo Americans. It was also much more difficult to obtain an entrée into this subculture and to determine its functional leadership and organizational structure. Finally we decided to emphasize the leadership aspects of the workshop rather than the parent-child relations content of the Project. Furthermore, in the case of Latin Americans our community contacts through businessmen and the churches proved more effective than the usual ones through the schools and PTA's. After several cancellations, false starts, and postponements, a successful workshop was held with Latin-American participants. Once under way, this workshop proved very successful and furnished an adequate supply of Latin-American leaders.

The further problem of selecting which prospects to train as leaders was one of considerable concern at the beginning of the Project. The obvious fact that not every person can be trained to be a successful discussion leader made some kind of selective procedure seem desirable. On the other hand, most of the prospects for the workshops were already leaders in the community in one capacity or another, and the unfavorable influence on the public relations of the Project that would accrue from rejecting an applicant seemed a high price to pay for the uncertain benefits of having a selection procedure. It also seemed likely, in view of our own lack of experience in training nonprofessional leaders, that we might unwittingly disqualify a few excellent prospects. With some trepidation, we decided to rely on a self-selection procedure. In effect, we felt that in most cases those persons who would not be suitable leaders would probably not be in sympathy with the basic philosophy of the workshop and would drop out. With the exception of only a handful of trainees, this proved to be the case. Moreover, additional protection lay in the fact that because a person completed a leader-training workshop did not automatically mean he would be used to lead a series. The assignment of leaders to discussion groups was the prerogative of the Project staff. As the workshops continued, our concern about selecting prospects diminished, for it became apparent that individuals who completed the training were, almost without exception, those who had the necessary qualities for discussion leadership. There was, of course, considerable variation in the effectiveness of the trained leaders; but the number of unsuitable prospects who went through the training was negligible.

The workshops followed a pattern of learning through experience. Each workshop was set up for a series of six weekly sessions. In nearly every instance additional meetings were scheduled, usually at the insistence of the participants. The workshops were all conducted by professionals,[1] the only phase of the educational portion of the Project in which specialists were involved. The first few meetings of each workshop were set up as discussion meetings themselves, with the trainees as participants. The director of the workshop would introduce a film on parent-child relations and then show the film to the group. An hour's discussion and a refreshment break followed. Then the director would analyze the discussion, sometimes with the help of observers and tape recorders.

After the first few meetings the workshop broke up into small groups after the film, with a trainee assuming the role of discussion leader. The director of the workshop moved from group to group, enabling the trainees to gain some early experience in leadership techniques while under his direct supervision and observation. Toward the end of the series the films used were on discussion leadership, rather than on parent-child relations, as stimulus for discussion and practice in leadership. Training manuals were used in all workshops, the first two using the St. Louis *Manual for Discussion Leadership*, and the remaining four a manual especially written for this Project.[2] Also available to the trainees was a small library of books on discussion leadership, but they availed them-

[1] See Appendix D, "Staff."

[2] Frank Cheavens, *Leading Group Discussions* (Austin, Texas, Hogg Foundation for Mental Health, University of Texas, 1958). See also, by the same author, *Developing Discussion Leaders in Brief Workshops* (Austin, Texas, Hogg Foundation for Mental Health, University of Texas, 1962).

selves of it very rarely. Apparently they were much more interested in learning by *doing* than by the more academic methods of study. In addition to the workshops themselves, a number of follow-up sessions were held so that all members of the various workshops could meet each other, preview films to be used in discussion groups, and discuss the leaders' experiences in the field. During most of this period the workshop director was available for individual consultation with leaders about their group-discussion activities; while some leaders took advantage of this opportunity, the majority did not. Individual consultation was, of course, worthwhile, but we did not consider it to be a crucial portion of the training.

An unsuccessful attempt was made during the first two workshops to study the leaders themselves by means of various measuring devices: a biographical inventory (developed from the Taylor Manifest Anxiety Scale), a Q-Sort of qualities of leadership, a sociometric analysis, and a leadership-role rating scale. All attempts at measurement met with resistance from workshop members. They were not particularly hostile toward these measurement attempts, but they were completely disinterested. It became apparent that our trainees had not come to serve as research subjects and were not interested in the over-all research aspects of the Project; they were concerned solely with developing their skills and talents as discussion leaders and giving volunteer service to the community through this means. Insufficient data were collected to make analysis possible, and this attempt at measurement was dropped rather than antagonize our leaders who were, of course, essential to the success of the Project.

Even without objective data on the leaders, it is possible to describe them in general terms by drawing upon several years' experience in working with them. The majority of them were women, although several extremely effective leaders were men. More men completed the leadership training than were able to serve, however, as they naturally had less time than women for volunteer services. It is worth noting that of our three best Latin-American leaders, two were men. In general, the educational level of the leaders was above average; most of them either had some college training, or had completed college. They tended to be active, successful people, and their experience with discussion leadership was usually not their first community service. All of them were married and, with very few exceptions, were parents. Perhaps the trait that was most universally present in our group of successful leaders was that of acceptance. They were not only willing but interested and objective listeners, with a genuine respect for the other person's point of view.

The amount of discussion leadership that trained leaders would undertake varied tremendously. Some of our "graduates" never consented to lead a series, although they felt that they themselves had profited greatly from attending the workshop. At the other extreme were those who gave this service high priority in the way they used their time and who amassed hundreds of hours of discussion leadership, both for the Project and in other community activities. With very few exceptions, leaders who undertook a discussion series were rewarded with considerable personal satisfaction. Not a single one asked to be relieved or replaced. Their reliability was really remarkable—in not a single instance, in four years of discussion meetings, did a leader fail to arrive at the meeting. However, since this was volunteer service, and since the best leaders were usually productive people, it was necessary to keep a fairly substantial pool of leaders available in order to staff our type of program. If, for example, plans called for conducting five discussion-group series simultaneously, then it was desirable to maintain a pool of from thirty to fifty trained people. It was also necessary to replenish the pool periodically by holding additional workshops, because of normal attrition factors (such as the members having commitments to other volunteer or civic activities, taking a job, or moving out of town).

Even those leaders who did not participate in the educational program itself, or who participated very slightly, became greater assets to the community. Most of these people were active in a wide variety of community organizations, and they applied to them the skill and training gained from the workshop, carrying the discussion techniques into church groups, school meetings, community welfare organizations, and Civil Defense classes. A strong case could be made for the value of leader-training workshops, as such, without their being attached to a community educational program. The workshop members represented at least a portion of community leadership and, to the extent that this leadership was made more effective, the community benefited.

IV

The Educational Program

THE EDUCATIONAL PROGRAM CHOSEN FOR THE PROJECT consisted of a series of six weekly meetings which would utilize group-discussion techniques under the guidance of a trained but nonprofessional leader. Educational films on various aspects of parent-child relations were to be shown at the beginning of each session to stimulate the discussion. With the basic decisions made as to the kind of educational program to be used, it was necessary to consider next what impact a project of this type would have on the community.

ADMINISTRATION AND FRAMEWORK OF THE PROGRAM

Obviously, an unwanted program cannot be imposed upon a community from the outside with any hope of success—and a program which is not designed to meet any felt need of the community is also doomed to failure. In the case of our Project, factors such as community acceptance and the felt need for improving parental education were particularly important, of course, since the discussion leaders, around whom the program was built, were to be recruited from people already in positions of community leadership. The second factor that made community acceptance of the Project imperative was the fact that the evaluative research which was to accompany the educational method, and which was an integral part of the Research Project, could be done only with the voluntary cooperation of a great many people in the community.

For these reasons, representatives of various community organizations were invited to share in our plans from the beginning. A Research Council,[1] formed at the inception of the Project, functioned as an advisory and policy board and included representatives from a number of organizations concerned with education in Austin.[2] This group was invaluable in the early stages of the Project in paving the way for community acceptance, as well as in providing consultation for both the research and educational aims of the Project.

In the initial developmental stages it was decided that the educational program and the research activities should be introduced separately to the community through existing local organizations. Accordingly, the Mental Health Association of Austin-Travis County was asked to serve as the community vehicle for introducing the educational program, and leadership-training workshops and the discussion groups became a regular part of its program. The Austin Community Guidance Center became the local sponsor for the research part of the Project, and was the agency for receiving funds granted the Project. The lay boards of both organizations were fully informed of proposed plans and gave the Project serious consideration before accepting it. Subsequently, the Mental Health Association held several open meetings to explain the purpose and operation of the Project to interested citizens. Acceptance of the Project by the lay boards of these two organizations undoubtedly had a very positive influence on its acceptance by the community.

These attempts to gain community support and acceptance were successful. The only serious opposition to the Project came from some members of Travis County Medical Association and was based in part on their apprehension that the discussion groups might provoke undue anxiety among parents and in part over concern that the groups were to be led by nonprofessionals. Perhaps the real reason for the opposition was that they were unconvinced that the purpose of the program was indeed educational rather than therapeutic. However, this opposition never reached an active stage and, in time, faded out entirely. In coping with this problem the help of the Director of the Community Guidance Center, himself

[1] See Appendix D, "Research Council."

[2] E.g., University of Texas, Hogg Foundation for Mental Health, Texas State Department of Health, Texas Education Agency, Austin Public Schools, Austin Community Guidance Center, Mental Health Association of Austin-Travis County, and Austin Congress of Parents and Teachers.

a psychiatrist, proved particularly valuable, for he served as a liaison between the Project and the physicians.

Since the administrative arrangement continued throughout the course of the Project, the leader-training workshops remained under the auspices of the Mental Health Association. In the beginning a full-time Director of Community Education was provided by the Project to direct these workshops and to organize the discussion groups for parents. Although paid by Project funds, he worked almost exclusively with the Mental Health Association as a member of its staff in furthering the educational program. During the last two years of operation, however, the educational portion of the Project became a function of the Mental Health Association in fact as well as in name. The duties of the Director of Community Education were taken over by the Executive Director of the Mental Health Association, who not only arranged the discussion groups for parents but also conducted the leader-training workshops. Originally, the educational program had derived its impetus from the Research Project; but ultimately it grew into a community endeavor and utilized resources that were available locally, regardless of whether or not formal research was being conducted.

The parent-discussion groups were organized through the respective elementary-school PTA's. Although some liaison work was necessary between the Research Project and the Austin Congress of Parents and Teachers, the actual contacts and arrangements were made through the individual elementary-school PTA's. Our educational program was never an integral part of the city-wide PTA arrangements. On the other hand, our program benefited greatly from the fact that a study-group program already existed in the Texas PTA organization. These study groups, held separately from the regular monthly PTA meetings, dealt with diverse subjects and used numerous educational methods. Material on such topics as parliamentary procedure, homemaking, home and family living, and mental health was available to the various PTA's. The study groups were usually planned for six weekly two-hour meetings, and a certificate was awarded to a member completing the twelve hours of study. This was the study-group format which was to be successfully utilized in carrying out our group-discussion program.

In the early years of the Project, it was necessary for the Director of Community Education (or a representative of the Mental Health Association) to get in touch with the chairman of the elementary-school PTA Committee on Mental Health or Home and Family Living and request that the Mental Health Association be allowed to cosponsor the existing framework of a PTA study group and employ the group-discussion method. Once the program became established, however, it was usually the PTA chairman who sought out the Mental Health Association to ask about the possibility of organizing a discussion-group program. In most instances, the planning phases included the representative from the Mental Health Association, the chairman of the PTA committee, the president of the school PTA (sometimes other officers as well), and usually the school principal. Undoubtedly this existing study-group framework greatly facilitated moving the discussion-group program into the community. Even though many PTA's had never had a study group of any kind, still the structure existed; and the idea of sponsoring an educational program that would award a certificate to persons who completed it had considerable appeal to many PTA officers and chairmen.

THE IMPORTANCE OF PUBLICITY

Despite the combined assets of community backing and approval and an existing framework through which the program could be carried out, the first attempt at a parent-discussion group led by a nonprofessional leader failed. The failure served to point up the extreme importance of publicity in connection with this kind of educational program. We learned two basic lessons from this first attempt: (1) attractive, interesting, and repeated publicity is necessary to induce a sufficient number of parents to register for a discussion group; (2) the publicity must be worded in such a way that it attracts the kind of parent who is able to adapt to, and profit from, the discussion-group approach. Keeping in mind what we had learned from the first attempt, we organized discussion groups in other schools throughout the city for four years without another failure.

The publicity for the initial study group was basically problem-oriented, as shown in Figure 1. This flier, which was sent home with all the students in the participating school, emphasized the problems of parent-child relations. In other words, this publicity unintentionally used what might be called a clinical rather than an educational approach. The parents who responded to this publicity were therefore those who

FIGURE 1

Example of Problem-oriented Publicity

STUDY GROUP IN PARENT-CHILD RELATIONS

Sponsored by the PTA and the Mental Health Society

shyness ?

anger ?

temper-tantrums ?

discipline ?

quarreling ?

eating ?

teasing ?

Comic books ?

homework ?

responsibility ?

allowance ?

bedtime ?

showing-off ?

whining ?

fears ?

TV ?

movies ?

playmates ?

friendships ?

homework ?

apron-strings ?

phases ?

daydreaming ?

you can help
and
be helped

in solving these and other problems

at the

STUDY GROUP IN
PARENT-CHILD RELATIONS

were having problems on, for the most part, a clinical level. These were parents who appeared to need therapy, not education, to work out their difficulties. Our publicity had unwittingly been directed at a level of parent-child disturbance which needed professional help. When the parents realized that the program was an educational one, directed by nonprofessionals, they quickly lost interest. Of the two groups organized through the use of the original publicity, one disbanded at the end of four meetings; the other, though continuing the full six sessions, wound up the last two meetings with only three or four participants.

After this mistake, the tenor of the publicity was changed to emphasize the educational aspects, fellowship, and informal atmosphere of the program (see Fig. 2). The effect of the revised publicity was remarkably obvious in the type of parent who then came to the discussion meetings. These parents had problems, of course, as do all parents, but with very few exceptions their problems were of a subclinical nature. It was necessary for the leaders of the group to refer only a few members to professionals for help. The revised publicity also made clear to the parents the purpose of the program, and there was very little chance of their feeling that they had been misled or misinformed (a feeling which had been distinctly present in the first group).

In addition to the need for changing the tenor of the publicity there was also a need to have more publicity, as indicated by the relatively small number of participants in the first school program. Thereafter we used the following schedule: the first flier went out from two to three weeks in advance of the first meeting; a second announcement followed about a week before the meeting; and parents received a third notice on the day before a discussion group was to begin. In some schools, a general reminder was also sent out after the first or second meeting had taken place, and post cards were mailed weekly to remind people who were attending the sessions; in a few schools, telephone committees assumed these final-reminder chores.

In all schools, one of the announcements (usually the first) was accompanied by a return post card which gave the parent the opportunity to register for the series. These registration cards served several purposes. From the point of view of the research design, it was essential for us to know in advance who was coming to the meetings so that measurements could be carried out before the program began. Furthermore, information on the card helped the organizers of the discussion group to

FIGURE 2

Example of Publicity Emphasizing the Educational and Discussion Aspects of the Program

DISCUSSION GROUP IN PARENT-CHILD RELATIONS

YOU ARE INVITED

to enroll in the

PALM P.T.A.
DISCUSSION GROUP

Films, Fun and Friends

Lots of information and learning about family living through

GROUP DISCUSSION

no formality - no lectures

no experts - no dues

Discussion Leaders will be Mr. Raymond Sanchez and Mr. Manuel Carmona

PARENT EDUCATION THROUGH GROUP DISCUSSION

HELPS PARENTS FIND WAYS

. . . of achieving greater happiness

. . . of getting along better together

. . . of understanding one another's viewpoints

estimate how many participants would prefer a morning or an evening meeting time, and how many participants would need child-care facilities. It was also necessary to know how many people would attend in order to provide an adequate number of leaders and appropriate physical facilities. In addition to these obvious purposes, the registration card served another purpose, less tangible but equally important: returning the card was an act of commitment. The parent who signs and returns a post card indicating that he will attend an educational program is far more likely to do so than one who merely makes a mental note to go. Parents are busy people, and self-educational programs do not often have a very high priority on the list of their activities, even though their interest and motivation may be fairly strong. Therefore, a device such as registration in advance, along with repeated publicity and reminders, is usually necessary to insure adequate attendance.

CONDUCTING THE DISCUSSION SESSIONS

In brief, the educational program consisted of a series of six two-hour weekly group-discussion meetings for parents, organized under the joint auspices of the Mental Health Association of Austin-Travis County and the elementary-school PTA, and using an existing study-group framework. Each meeting was conducted by a trained but nonprofessional discussion leader. With a few exceptions, meetings began with an educational film on parent-child relations, the primary purpose of which was to stimulate discussion and provide a general topic for the meeting. In several instances, brief plays or skits were used in place of the film.[3] A few groups requested, after the preliminary meetings, that no stimulus at all be used, as they preferred to use the entire time for discussion. The meetings were held in a variety of places, the selection being determined by suitability and convenience. In the majority of cases a room in the school building was used, but meetings were also held in churches, Boy Scout huts, and in homes. Refreshments, usually of a simple type such as coffee and cookies, were served at almost all the meetings, at whatever time the group preferred to take a break. Responsibility for providing refreshments also varied; sometimes it was assumed by the Mental Health Association, sometimes by the PTA, and sometimes by members of the

[3] Appendix C contains a list of these films and plays.

group. The meetings were uniformly scheduled to last two hours, and this time limit was adhered to rather strictly, with responsibility for staying within the allotted period resting upon the discussion leader.

The discussion groups were highly acceptable to the participants. Parents enjoyed the meetings and seemed to feel that this kind of learning was fun. The atmosphere was informal, and most of the discussions were punctuated frequently by laughter. Moreover, some lasting friendships were reported to have been formed at the meetings. The humor and informality did not mean that the groups were superficial or social in nature, however. Leaders noted repeatedly that parents discussed topics which were a source of great personal anxiety, and that these discussions were on a serious level. Many leaders and observers expressed astonishment not only at how quickly parents began discussing, with frankness and openness, those problems which were of genuine concern, but also at the depth of emotion and feeling often shown by these parents. Although the group discussions were apparently a very palatable form of education, they were by no means casual. Many husbands or wives who attended meetings alone mentioned that they usually gave a detailed report of the discussion to their spouses.

Years of experience with these discussion groups resulted in a considerable amount of "know-how" in techniques for promoting their successful operation.[4] As already noted, the content and frequency of publicity and the device of preregistration were among the vital factors. The physical facilities for the meeting were also important. Flexibility of seating arrangements was particularly essential here, for participants in a discussion meeting should be seated in a circle so that everyone, including the leader, can see and hear everyone else. The size of the meeting place was also of significance. For example, using the corner of a vast room or auditorium for a small group of people was especially disadvantageous; the group felt dwarfed and voices were lost. Experience showed that a comfortable and informal room should be selected, and that disturbing influences should be minimized. Children can be particularly distracting to parent groups, so child-care facilities were almost al-

[4] Carl F. Hereford, *Organizing Group Discussions* (Austin, Texas, Hogg Foundation for Mental Health, University of Texas, 1961). This pamphlet is designed specifically for persons wishing to plan an educational program which will employ group-discussion methods.

FIGURE 3

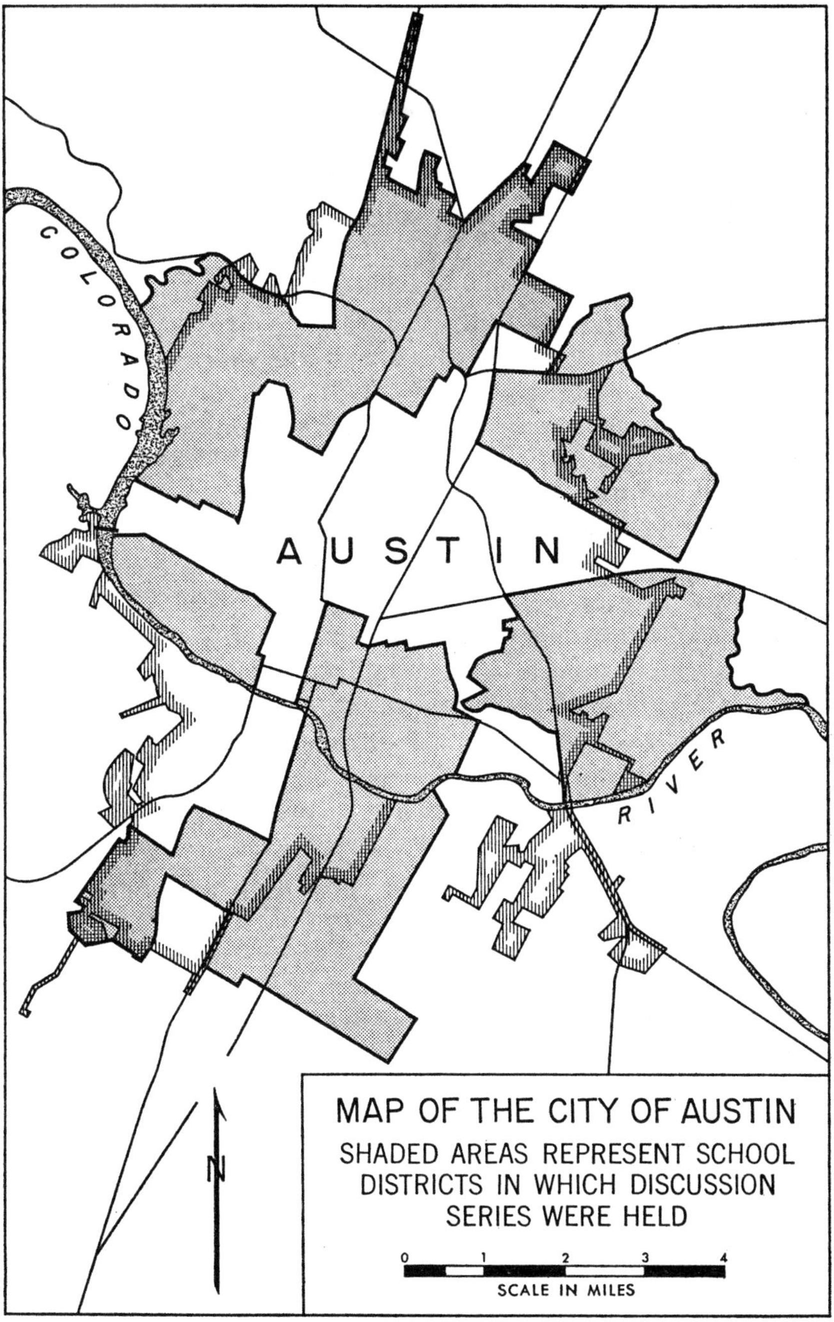
COLORADO
AUSTIN
RIVER
N
MAP OF THE CITY OF AUSTIN
SHADED AREAS REPRESENT SCHOOL DISTRICTS IN WHICH DISCUSSION SERIES WERE HELD
0 1 2 3 4
SCALE IN MILES

ways provided. If this was not possible, it was clearly understood that parents were not to bring their children with them. When child-care facilities were provided, they were far enough away that the parents could not hear the children. There is probably nothing more disturbing to a group of mothers than the sound of a child crying.

The film used as a stimulus for discussion deserves mention, although our experience with the groups indicated that the quality of the film is not crucial to the ensuing conversation; indeed, many groups did not discuss the film at all, although they talked for an hour and a half about the same topic as that covered by the film. While the films undoubtedly did have some value as discussion stimuli, our experience indicated that an equal if not greater value may lie in the fact that they provided a common experiential background for the group—a particularly important condition in the early meetings. After the parents had seen the same film they had something in common, even though they were relative strangers. This shared experience increased group cohesiveness and facilitated discussion, whether the conversation itself centered on the film or not.

Experience with these groups showed that films should always be previewed, at least by the discussion leader and preferably by all those connected with organizing the group, as many film titles and catalogue descriptions are incomplete or misleading. Preparations for showing the film are important, too. The equipment should be set up and tested before the meeting, and of course a qualified operator must be on hand. Careful advance planning is essential in all arrangements for the meeting. Adult education, especially when organized on a volunteer basis, has suffered greatly from lack of attention to the small but important details of organization and execution that insure a smooth and effective meeting.

Using the procedures and techniques described here, thirty discussion-group series[5] were carried out in fifteen schools over a period of four years under the auspices of the Research Project; it was on data concerning these groups that the research findings were based. The school districts covered the city of Austin quite well geographically (see Fig. 3), and in-

[5] In all, 22 leaders were used for these meetings, each leader having conducted an average of 1.5 series, with a range of 1 to 5 (a few of the meetings had coleaders). The combined attendance at all these discussion series was 916 parents—a mean of 30.5 parents per series, with a range of 10 to 46. Not all parents attended every meeting of the series, however; the number at any one meeting was usually about 15.

cluded brand-new school districts as well as the old established ones. These districts also covered the socioeconomic range found in this city, as well as the two ethnic minorities, the Negro and the Latin American. In terms of acceptance, the discussion method worked well all across the range on the various dimensions under consideration. There were more organizational problems at the lower socioeconomic level and with the Latin-American groups; but, once started, the discussion groups in these school districts were just as successful as those in the other districts.

V

The Research Design

Evaluative research on any kind of action program designed to influence human behavior in its natural or real-life setting is beset by many pitfalls. Research methodology, when stripped to the essentials, is clearly a product of the laboratory, not of the community. It is based on control of variables, uniformity of subjects, and standardization of the experimental variable under study. Not one of these conditions is precisely met when real-life situations become the setting for research. It may be that this inherent weakness is responsible for the questionable value of much of the research that has been done in parent education. For example, programs are considered to be effective and successful if they are well attended or if a majority of the participants fill out a questionnaire about the program in a positive vein. Evaluative research is time-consuming and expensive; yet the demand by parents for educational service is so strong that the tendency has been to go ahead and meet the demand in any way possible, regardless of the dearth of knowledge concerning the effectiveness of the techniques used.

Although present research methodology in the area under discussion fits the nonlaboratory situation only imperfectly, it can be modified to achieve meaningful results. Among other features, such evaluative research in the community must include three essentials if the findings are to be clearly interpretable: (*a*) a large sample; (*b*) control cases against which to evaluate the main effects of the program; and (*c*) thorough statistical analysis of the variable employed. That is to say, the research sample must be large enough that sporadic or chance variables among the subjects will cancel out. Control groups receiving treatment different from the experimental group (or no treatment at all) must be used to give reasonable assurance that changes noted are related to the experimental variable under study and not to some other extraneous and perhaps unknown factor. Finally, analysis of the data must be rigorous enough statistically to account for interaction among important variables.

MAJOR ELEMENTS OF THE DESIGN

Since not all relevant variables can be controlled, a research design (see Fig. 4) which would cover as many of these variables as possible had to be established. The eventual design was made up of one main group—Experimental—and three control groups—Lecture, Nonattendant, and Random—plus the measurements for each group taken both before and after the educational program.

In these four categories the basic unit of measurement was the individual parent and his children. The educational program did not reach the children directly; they were assigned to groups according to the placement of their parents. The typical research period corresponded roughly to a school semester. All initial measurements for all research groups were carried out during the week before the parent-discussion groups were to begin in a given school, and the final measurements were taken from about four to six weeks after the last of the six weekly discussion meetings. The initial-to-final research interval was, therefore, about three months. A total of seven such research periods covered a span of four years. During these periods the subjects for all groups (with the exception of the members of the Lecture-Control Group) were drawn from the respective school with which they were affiliated; and several schools always participated in the programs simultaneously. Drawing subjects from the same school at the same time was desirable in that it tended to equate the groups and, at least in a general sense, to make sure that their exposure to nonexperimental variables was approximately the same.

The four main categories were classified as follows:

Experimental Group (parents who attended at least one meeting of a discussion-group series).

FIGURE 4

Chart of Typical Research Period

CATEGORIES	RESEARCH PERIOD				
	Initial Measurements		Intervening Method of Education	Final Measurements	
	For Parents	For Children		For Parents	For Children
Experimental Group: composed of parents[1] who attended a discussion-group series	Parent-Attitude Survey and Parent Interview	Sociometric Evaluation and Teacher Rating	Discussion-Group Series	(Same as in the Initial Measurements)	(Same as in the Initial Measurements)
Lecture-Control Group: composed of parents[1] who attended a lecture series			Lecture Series		
Nonattendant-Control Group: composed of parents[1] who registered for an educational program but did not attend			None		
Random-Control Group: composed of parents[1] whose names were selected at random from the school files					

[1] And their children (children received no experimental treatment).

Lecture-Control Group (parents who did not participate in a discussion-group series but who did attend at least one of a series of lectures by professionals in the field of parent-child relations).

To minimize differences due to socioeconomic or ethnic factors, the lecture series were held in schools where discussion groups had been organized, but at a later date. Parents who had attended previous discussion series were eliminated as subjects for the Lecture-Control Group. A lecture series was organized in the same manner as the discussion-group program; that is, it was sponsored by the PTA and the Mental Health Association and consisted of six weekly meetings of approximately two hours each. Neither the lecturer nor the audience was aware of their control status. The lecturers were drawn from professionals in the community, and included psychologists, social workers, pediatricians, educators, ministers, psychiatrists, and juvenile authorities. The lecturers were not instructed as to what method or technique to use, but they were assigned a topic in keeping with the subject of the films used in the discussion groups. The lecturers were paid a small honorarium.

Nonattendant-Control Group (parents who registered for either a discussion group or a lecture series but did not attend).

This group was designed, primarily, to control "volunteer" bias. The fact that the parents failed to attend is evidence that they are not strictly comparable to those in the Experimental Group, even though the two groups showed some similarity in that both had originally registered for the meetings. It was not possible to determine, in general terms, the reason for nonattendance in this group. In many instances, however, nonattendance was known to be based on factors that seemed irrelevant to the variable under study, such as illness in the family, or conflicting engagements.

Random-Control Group (parents who did not register for or attend either the discussion group or the lecture series).

This group was selected at random from the alphabetical lists in the school files after first eliminating those who were already included in one of the other categories.

In the course of the Research Project, almost half of the elementary-school districts in Austin were utilized. School districts were selected partly on the basis of requests from the PTA of a particular district for the educational programs, and partly on the basis of our need for representative geographic, socioeconomic, and ethnic coverage. As already mentioned, in some instances, particularly with the lower socioeconomic districts and the Latin-American districts, members of the Mental Health Association took the initiative in making contact with the PTA in order to organize the discussion groups. To assure adequate coverage for our research purposes, the Mental Health Association provided not only the leader and consultation services but also whatever help was necessary to get the program under way in a given PTA. In almost all instances, this help included mimeographing publicity releases for the program, and in some instances, it included help for such expenses as custodian fees, child care, and occasionally the cost of refreshments. Furthermore, the Mental Health Association provided the films from the film library of the Texas State Health Department, although selection of the films was usually made in collaboration with the PTA. It also made available a motion-picture projector to those PTA's which did not have one.

To provide a framework for evaluating the group-discussion method of parental education, the following hypothetical schema of the impact of this method on the individual parent was constructed.

Attendance at a series of group-discussion meetings on parent-child relations moderated by a trained but nonprofessional leader provides the parent with an opportunity for more

Participation in the discussion. This participation by the parent, plus the climate of freedom, acceptance, and sharing of experiences and ideas provided by the group, leads to more

Personal involvement of the parent. This participation and involvement of the parent in the group discussions brings about changes in

Parental attitudes regarding parent-child relations and child-rearing practices. These attitudinal changes lead to

Behavioral changes on the part of the parent, which, through the parent-child interaction, lead to changes in the

Child's behavior in his relations and activities at school.

THE AREAS OF MEASUREMENT

The research measurements were designed to test this sequential framework at its various stages. Since it was manifestly impossible to measure *all* areas of parental attitudes and behavior, limited ones had to be selected for study. These choices, made by a subcommittee of the Research Council,[1] were based on a triple prerequisite: the area had to be important to parent-child relations, measurable, and receptive to influence by educational methods. This three-pronged requirement yielded seven areas to be measured. Of these, five concern parental attitudes and behavior, and two concern child behavior.

Confidence in Parental Role

This scale refers to the parent's concept of himself.

In terms of a continuum, the attitude ranges from the low end—at which a parent feels inadequate, dissatisfied, and unsure, and believes that he lacks the ability to be a good parent—to the opposite end—at which a parent feels sure of himself, adequate to meet the demands of parenthood, and unconcerned about the difficulties of parent-child relations.

Causation of Child's Behavior

This scale is concerned with the interpretation a parent makes of his child's behavior, and the extent to which he involves himself as a causative factor.

At one end of this continuum is the parent who holds that behavior is inherited or due to supernatural factors, or who takes the position of immutable causal determinism. At the other end is the parent who feels his child's behavior is determined by parent-child interaction, by environmental influences, and by parental behavior and attitudes.

Acceptance of Child's Behavior and Feelings

This scale measures the degree to which a parent is satisfied with his child, finds that the child's behavior fits in with his own concepts, and sees the child as an individual in his own right.

At one end of this continuum is the parent who overtly and completely rejects his child. At the other end is the completely permissive parent.

Mutual Understanding

This scale might almost be thought of as a communication or interaction variable, although it is not necessarily dependent on the amount of verbal exchange.

[1] This committee was comprised of O. H. Bown, W. H. Holtzman, Carson McGuire, Harry Moore, and Philip Worchel. See Appendix D, "Research Council."

At the lower end of this continuum is the parent who does not share ideas, attitudes, or feelings with his child; at the upper end is the parent who prizes the reciprocal exchange of both the intellectual and emotional aspects of living.

Mutual Trust

This scale measures the amount of confidence that parents and children have in each other.

At the lower end of this continuum is a parent-child relation marked by suspicion and deceit; at the other end is a relation characterized by mutual confidence and trust.

In addition to the five foregoing scales of parental attitudes and behavior, two important areas of child behavior were also selected for testing. Areas outside parent-child relations were selected for these tests in order to provide an independent test of the effect of the experimental variable.

Classmate Relations

The social acceptability of the child is tested by the question: "How well is the child accepted by his peers?"

At the lower end of this continuum is the child who is an isolate, who does not participate in social activities, who is never chosen by the other children. At the upper end is the child who is popular, well-liked and included by his peers in their activities.

Classroom Adjustment

The child's adjustment to the most important social situation in which he finds himself outside the home—his classroom—is the subject with which this scale is concerned.

The rating of this adjustment was made by his teacher, the adult who, with the exception of the child's parents, is likely to know the most about him. At the lower end of this continuum is the child whom his teacher sees as making a poor adjustment to the classroom setting; at the upper end is the child who his teacher feels is making a good adjustment.

Measurements in these attitudinal and behavioral areas were taken on persons in all the categories in order to test the last three sections of the hypothetical framework—Parental Attitudes, Behavioral Changes, and

Child's Behavior. Moreover, records on the first three areas—Attendance, Participation, and Personal Involvement—were kept by observers for the Experimental Group. These observers, who attended every meeting of each discussion series, were there ostensibly to check attendance and operate the motion-picture projector. No effort was made, however, to conceal the fact that they were also keeping records of the discussion. The observers were told to keep a tally not only of the number of actual verbal comments but also of the number of personal references made by each participant.[2] These detailed records made it possible to include the variables of attendance, participation, and personal involvement in the data analyzed.

Using the dimensions of attitudes and behavior for both parents and children, in conjunction with the records of the quantity and nature of participation of parents in the discussion group, we made certain predictions or constructed two operational hypotheses:

Hypothesis I. Parents who attend a series of meetings on parent-child relations in which the group-discussion technique is used will show positive movement or change in the measurements of the attitudinal and behavioral dimensions. Children of these parents, although not directly involved in the group-discussion program, will also show positive movement or change in the measurements of the dimensions of child behavior. This change will manifest itself reliably in groups, but may show considerable variance among individuals.

Positive movement or change on the part of parents (and their children) will be greater in the case of participants in the discussion groups than in the case of participants in the Lecture Group, Nonattendant Group, or Random-Control Group.

Hypothesis II. The number of discussion meetings attended, the quantity of participation, the frequency of personal references—all will be positively related to the degree of positive change in parents who attended the discussion group.

[2] See Appendix A, "Instructions to Observers."

VI

The Measuring Instruments

THE MEASURING INSTRUMENTS, CONSTRUCTED SPECIFICALLY for this Project, were designed to measure the dimensions of attitudes and behavior, the subject of the preceding chapter. In addition to meeting the usual measurement requirements, these instruments had to yield scores which would be comparable for subjects from various research groups (or categories) in the different schools used in the Project.

Each instrument was developed, tested on a preliminary group, and then revised for final use. Where appropriate, reliabilities and interrelations of the instruments were determined. Two instruments were developed for use with parents: a set of five attitude scales, and an individual interview schedule. Two measuring devices were also constructed for use with children: a sociometric evaluation, and ratings by the children's teachers.

The development, testing, and functions of the four instruments used in the Project are described here. The various forms and instructions for these instruments are reproduced in Appendix A.

RESEARCH ON PARENTS

PARENT-ATTITUDE SURVEY

Development of the Scales. Scales were constructed to measure parent attitudes in the five areas selected by the subcommittee of the Research Council—*confidence* in the parental role, *causation* of the child's behavior, *acceptance* of the child's behavior and feelings, mutual *understanding*, and mutual *trust*. From similar instruments we borrowed items appropriate to the areas under study. When not enough suitable items could be located in previous work, new items were written by the Project staff. The original pool contained more than 200 items, approximately 40 for each area. These were classified according to their appropriateness for the respective areas by five judges[1] working independently of each other. A sixth area—unclassifiable—was provided for those items the judges considered to be either ambiguous or unrelated to any of the five basic areas in question. Each judge was given a description of the attitude area and a stack of thoroughly shuffled cards with one item on each. The judge was asked to place each item in the attitude area to which he felt it most closely pertained.

Through this method 25 items for each area were selected. The majority of these items showed 100 per cent agreement among the judges, and the remainder, with but few exceptions, won agreement from four of the five judges. No item was adopted unless at least three of the judges agreed on its placement.

The 125 items became the preliminary form of the attitude scales and were tested on 72 parents (16 from Harris School in Austin and 56 from the three elementary schools in Taylor, Texas). Each item consisted of a statement for which the parent marked one of five choices: Strongly Agree, Agree, Undecided, Disagree, or Strongly Disagree. The extremes of this five-point scale were scored +2 or −2, depending on whether the item was stated positively or negatively. Likewise the Agree and Disagree choices were scored +1 or −1; the Undecided response was scored zero. The algebraic sum of the item scores in each area served as the parent's total score for that attitude area. Each parent therefore received five separate scores, one for each scale.

The next step was to refine and shorten these scales by determining the discriminatory power of each item for its particular scale. To insure greater homogeneity of content in each scale, items were retained in which both the item score and the total scale score were high or low for the same subject. Items were eliminated when there was no relation be-

[1] Frank Cheavens, Charles Dent, Wayne Holtzman, Paul Rothaus, and Carl Hereford.

tween the item score and the total scale score. The discrimination index employed for item selection consisted of the product-moment correlation coefficient between each item and its total scale score, with the standardization group of 72 parents being used as subjects. A high correlation coefficient indicated that the item score was closely related to the total scale score, and a low correlation, of course, showed little relationship between them.

The 15 items with the highest correlation coefficients in each of the five areas were used in the final version of the Parent-Attitude Survey, making a total of 75 items. The decision to limit the number of items to 15 per scale was a compromise between the need for reliability (the longer the scale, the greater its reliability) and the necessity to keep to a reasonable period the amount of time required by the subjects to check all the statements. Most parents were able to complete the Parent-Attitude Survey in fifteen or twenty minutes.

To put the subjects at ease, we made every effort to phrase the items in simple and colloquial (even ungrammatical, at times) language. The fact that they were written in a conversational style—as natural expressions of thought, not as formal statements—also maximized the likelihood that each statement would be clearly understood by all the subjects, including those from the ethnic minorities and those from the lower socioeconomic levels.

The items used in the final form of the scales, as well as those eliminated,[2] are presented in Tables 1–5. In general, items which were negatively phrased (that is, where agreement with the statement received a low score and vice versa) proved to have the highest item-scale correlation. In the original pool of some 200 items the proportion of positive and negative items was about equal, but most of the positively phrased ones

[2] The sources of 52 of the 75 items used in the final form of the Parent-Attitude Survey are: E. S. Schaefer and R. Q. Bell, *Parental Attitude Research Instrument* (Bethesda, Maryland, National Institute for Mental Health). Mimeograph [39 items]; J. C. Glidewell, I. N. Mensh, H. R. Domke, Margaret C.-L. Gildea, and A. D. Buchmueller, "Methods for Community Mental Health Research," *American Journal of Orthopsychiatry*, Vol. 27 (1957), pp. 38–54 [5 items]; Jane Loevinger and Blanche Sweet, "Family Problems Scale" (St. Louis, Missouri, St. Louis Jewish Hospital, unpublished) [4 items]; J. Pierce-Jones, *Parent Attitude Survey* (Austin, Texas, Department of Educational Psychology, University of Texas). Mimeograph [3 items]; I. S. Shapiro, "Parent Attitude Questionnaire" (New York, Health Insurance Plan of Greater New York, unpublished) [1 item]. The Project staff provided 23 new items.

were subsequently eliminated by the judges in the course of the content sorting or by the item-scale correlation method. Some of the items were discarded by the latter method because of little or no "spread" in the responses; that is, since almost all the parents answered the statement in the same way, the correlation between item and scale was low. Some of the other items that were omitted had a sufficient span of responses, but as these responses were not related to the total scale score, a low correlation again resulted.

TABLE 1

Parent-Attitude Survey Scale No. 1: *Confidence*

Item Number[1]	*Item Content*	*Item Direction*[2]	*Item-Scale Correlation*
38	I feel I am faced with more problems than most parents.	—	.80
53	Few parents have to face the problems I find with my children.	—	.79
23	It's hard to know what to do when a child is afraid of something that won't hurt him.	—	.73
18	Most parents aren't sure what is the best way to bring up children.	—	.71
48	Children don't realize that it mainly takes suffering to be a good parent.	—	.68
33	Parents sacrifice most of their fun for their children.	—	.67
28	Raising children isn't as hard as most parents let on.	+	.65
58	It's hard to know when to make a rule and stick by it.	—	.61
73	Raising children is a nerve-wracking job.	—	.57
68	It's hard to know what healthy sex ideas are.	—	.54
63	A parent has to suffer much and say little.	—	.48
43	It's hard to know whether to be playful rather than dignified with children.	—	.45

TABLE 1—Continued

Parent-Attitude Survey Scale No. 1: *Confidence*

Item Number[1]	*Item Content*	*Item Direction*[2]	*Item-Scale Correlation*
13	It's a rare parent who can be even-tempered with the children all day.	—	.45
8	Fewer people are doing a good job of child-rearing now than 30 years ago.	—	.41
3	Taking care of a small baby is something that no woman should be expected to do all by herself.	—	.40
	Parents are frequently puzzled by the things their children do.	—	.38
	More people are doing a good job of raising children today than 30 years ago.	+	.37
	Most parents know instinctively what is the best way to bring up children.	+	.26
	Parents who start a child talking about his worries don't realize that they may get into something they can't handle.	—	.24
	If parents would rely more on common sense there wouldn't be so much fuss about the best way to raise children.	+	.20
1	Parents have to sacrifice everything for their children.[3]	—	.20
	Most parents wonder if they are as good as the parents of other children in the neighborhood.	—	.18
	Probably no parent is sure just how to meet all the problems that he has.	—	.15
	To take care of their children parents must neglect their own welfare.	—	.12
	Most parents believe they are a little better than the parents of other children in the neighborhood.	+	.11

[1] Unnumbered items were omitted from the final form of the scale.

[2] A plus sign indicates that agreement with the statement received a positive score; a minus sign indicates that agreement with the statement received a negative score.

[3] This was a buffer item and was not scored as part of the scale.

TABLE 2

Parent-Attitude Survey Scale No. 2: *Causation*

Item Number[1]	*Item Content*	*Item Direction*[a]	*Item-Scale Correlation*
74	Some children are just naturally bad.	—	.86
49	Some children are so naturally headstrong that a parent can't really do much about them.	—	.84
64	If a child is born bad there's not much you can do about it.	—	.80
4	When you come right down to it, a child is either good or bad and there's not much you can do about it.	—	.79
54	Why children behave the way they do is too much for anyone to figure out.	—	.73
69	A child is destined to be a certain kind of person no matter what the parents do.	—	.71
44	A child that comes from bad stock doesn't have much chance of amounting to anything.	—	.68
39	Most of the bad traits children have (like nervousness or bad temper) are inherited.	—	.64
9	With all a child hears at school and from friends, there's little a parent can do to influence him.	—	.60
14	Psychologists now know that what a child is born with determines the kind of person he becomes.	—	.58
24	Most all children are just the same at birth; it's what happens to them afterwards that is important.	+	.56
19	A child may learn to be a juvenile delinquent from playing games like cops and robbers and war too much.	—	.50
29	There are many things that influence a young child that parents don't understand and can't do anything about.	—	.50

TABLE 2—Continued

Parent-Attitude Survey Scale No. 2: *Causation*

Item Number[1]	*Item Content*	*Item Direction*[2]	*Item-Scale Correlation*
34	Many times parents are punished for their own sins through the bad behavior of their children.	—	.43
59	Not even psychologists understand exactly why children act the way they do.	—	.38
	If children dislike certain foods, it is often because a parent dislikes these same foods.	+	.34
	A child will turn out just about the same no matter what you think you are teaching him.	—	.33
	No matter what parents try to do, there are children who don't change at all in the way they behave.	—	.30
	It is now known that most of children's behavior problems are caused by parents.	+	.28
	If children get into difficulty, it is mainly because their parents do not love them enough.	+	.25
	If a child turns out bad, you can bet it's the fault of the parents.	+	.23
	The way a child grows up is determined by the parents' attitudes and behavior.	+	.20
	Heredity plays a much more important part in a child's development than environment.	—	.18
	Problems in children come out of troubles inside the family.	+	.16
	Children are born without any fears or worries, so those that develop must be the parents' fault.	+	.16

[1] Unnumbered items were omitted from the final form of the scale.

[2] A plus sign indicates that agreement with the statement received a positive score; a minus sign indicates that agreement with the statement received a negative score.

TABLE 3

Parent-Attitude Survey Scale No. 3: *Acceptance*

Item Number[1]	*Item Content*	*Item Direction*[2]	*Item-Scale Correlation*
5	The earlier a child is weaned from its emotional ties to its parents the better it will handle its own problems.	—	.68
40	A child who misbehaves should be made to feel guilty and ashamed of himself.	—	.68
20	There is no reason why a child should not learn to keep his clothes clean very early in life.	—	.65
60	Children should be toilet-trained at the earliest possible time.	—	.63
30	A child who wants too much affection may become a "softie" if it is given to him.	—	.61
50	One thing I cannot stand is a child's constantly wanting to be held.	—	.59
45	A child should be weaned away from the bottle or breast as soon as possible.	—	.58
70	It's a parent's right to refuse to put up with a child's annoyances.	—	.53
35	If you put too many restrictions on a child, you will stunt his personality.	+	.53
55	When a boy is cowardly, he should be forced to try things he is afraid of.	—	.48
25	Playing with a baby too much should be avoided since it excites them and they won't sleep.	—	.45
75	A child should be taught to avoid fighting no matter what happens.	—	.39
15	One reason that it is sad to see children grow up is because they need you more when they are babies.	—	.37
10	If a little girl is a tomboy, her mother should try to get her interested in dolls and playing house.	—	.37

TABLE 3—Continued

Parent-Attitude Survey Scale No. 3: *Acceptance*

Item Number[1]	*Item Content*	*Item Direction*[2]	*Item-Scale Correlation*
65	There's no acceptable excuse for a child hitting another child.	—	.34
	When children seem hard to put up with, parents should remember that all children need to misbehave sometime.	+	.32
	A five-year-old needs to be picked up and cuddled once in a while.	+	.28
	A baby really doesn't appreciate or enjoy the babytalk or attention of adults half as much as parents think.	—	.27
	Even though it is hard, a parent should let a child have its own way so that it can develop independence.	+	.18
	A parent has to be constantly alert to meet all the needs of a growing child.	+	.15
	Most parents prefer a quiet child to a "scrappy" one.	—	.12
	Basically, children are just small adults and should be treated as such if they do wrong.	—	.09
2	Parents should help children feel they belong and are needed.[3]	+	.07
	Parents should recognize that children have a lot of things to do that are pretty important to them.	+	.07
	The sooner a child learns to walk, the better he is trained.	—	.05

[1] Unnumbered items were omitted from the final form of the scale.

[2] A plus sign indicates that agreement with the statement received a positive score; a minus sign indicates that agreement with the statement received a negative score.

[3] This was a buffer item and was not scored as part of the scale.

TABLE 4

Parent-Attitude Survey Scale No. 4: *Understanding*

Item Number[1]	*Item Content*	*Item Direction*[2]	*Item-Scale Correlation*
31	Family life would be happier if parents made children feel they were free to say what they think about anything.	+	.81
71	Talking with a child about his fears most often makes the fear look more important than it is.	—	.78
51	A child's ideas should be seriously considered in making family decisions.	+	.74
66	Children should have a share in making family decisions just as the grown-ups do.	+	.73
56	If you let children talk about their troubles they end up complaining even more.	—	.72
26	Children shouldn't be asked to do all the compromising without a chance to express their side of things.	+	.70
46	There's a lot of truth in the saying, "Children should be seen and not heard."	—	.68
41	Family conferences which include the children don't usually accomplish much.	—	.65
36	Most children's fears are so unreasonable it only makes things worse to let the child talk about them.	—	.65
16	The trouble with trying to understand children's problems is they usually just make up a lot of stories to keep you interested.	—	.64
61	A child should always accept the decision of his parents.	—	.51
21	If a parent sees that a child is right and the parent is wrong, they should admit it and try to do something about it.	+	.48
76	Children don't try to understand their parents.	—	.45

TABLE 4—Continued

Parent-Attitude Survey Scale No. 4: *Understanding*

Item Number[1]	*Item Content*	*Item Direction*[2]	*Item-Scale Correlation*
11	A child has a right to his own point of view and ought to be allowed to express it, just as parents express theirs.	+	.40
6	Most of the time giving advice to children is a waste of time because they either don't take it or don't need it.	—	.38
	Children should be encouraged to express their opinions about anything which involves them.	+	.35
	Children should be encouraged to tell their parents about it whenever they feel family rules are unreasonable.	+	.33
	A parent who tries to talk over every little problem may find his children are just trying to get out of doing things.	—	.27
	Laughing at children's jokes and telling children jokes helps families to get along better.	+	.22
	There is no reason parents should have their own way all the time, any more than children should have their own way all the time.	+	.18
	When you do things together, children feel close to you and can talk easier.	+	.16
	Children should always feel their parents are interested in what happens to them.	+	.15
	Parents need to do things with children so there will be other things to talk about besides telling them what is wrong, what they must do, etc.	+	.12
	Parents should be interested in hearing about their children's parties and fun.	+	.12
	It is good for parents to develop a close feeling with their children by sharing experiences with them.	+	.10

[1] Unnumbered items were omitted from the final form of the scale.

[2] A plus sign indicates that agreement with the statement received a positive score; a minus sign indicates that agreement with the statement received a negative score.

TABLE 5

Parent-Attitude Survey Scale No. 5: *Trust*

Item Number[1]	*Item Content*	*Item Direction*[2]	*Item-Scale Correlation*
67	Children who are not watched will get in trouble.	—	.75
32	Children must be told exactly what to do and how to do it or they will make mistakes.	—	.73
72	Children have no right to keep anything from their parents.	—	.67
62	Children have a right to activities which do not include their parents.	+	.64
22	A child should be allowed to try out what it can do at times without the parents watching.	+	.59
52	More parents should make it their job to know everything their child is doing.	—	.55
47	If rules are not closely enforced children will misbehave and get into trouble.	—	.55
7	It is hard to let children go and visit people because they might misbehave when parents aren't around.	—	.51
37	It is hard to know when to let boys and girls play together when they can't be seen.	—	.48
77	A child should never keep a secret from his parents.	—	.44
27	Parents should make it their business to know everything their children are thinking.	—	.43
57	An alert parent should try to learn all his child's thoughts.	—	.38
17	A mother has a right to know everything going on in her child's life because her child is a part of her.	—	.34
12	If children are quiet for a while you should immediately find out why.	—	.28
42	It's a parent's duty to make sure he knows a child's innermost thoughts.	—	.24
	Children should be trusted to spend their allowances as they want even if it seems foolish to parents.	+	.22

TABLE 5—Continued

Parent-Attitude Survey Scale No. 5: *Trust*

Item Number[1]	*Item Content*	*Item Direction*[2]	*Item-Scale Correlation*
	A child who is kept busy will not get into mischief.	—	.18
	Children should be given a chance to try out as many things on their own as possible.	+	.18
	The experience of being on their own is often good for children.	+	.17
	Children and parents may fuss a lot, but when the chips are down, they can count on each other.	+	.14
	If children are to grow up and get somewhere in life, parents must keep after them all the time.	—	.10
	Parents and children can feel close without always being in each other's company.	+	.08
	Working alone and without help is often a very satisfying experience for a child.	+	.07
	A child needs some privacy, so parents should cooperate by giving him some time to himself.	+	.07
	If a parent is not careful a child may be thinking things he does not know about.	—	.05

[1] Unnumbered items were omitted from the final form of the scale.

[2] A plus sign indicates that agreement with the statement received a positive score; a minus sign indicates that agreement with the statement received a negative score.

How well did the items finally selected conform to the dimensions of parental attitudes defined in the research design? A study of the content of the items with the highest item-scale correlations showed that the five scales appeared to fit their predicted dimensions fairly closely.

The items in the first scale, *Confidence,* that have the highest correlations are those concerned with the parent's feeling that he has more problems than most parents, and those concerned with an attitude of uncertainty and unsureness as to what to do about these problems. Also high in the order of discriminatory power are items which either say or imply that being a parent requires suffering and sacrifice. Another major block is composed of those items which indicate that being a parent is a difficult, time-consuming, thankless task.

Causation, the second scale, measures the dimension of natural or inherent causation as contrasted to environmental or parental influence. Most of the high correlations here are for items that emphasize the impossibility of changing a child from the way he is "naturally." Another type of item which predominates in this scale suggests that the behavior of the child, though incomprehensible, is predetermined.

The third scale, *Acceptance*, is less clearly defined than the others. Some of the items carry the idea of "pushing" the child, that is, of not accepting childhood behavior. But present, too, are statements that indicate parental reluctance to accept normal developmental changes in the child. Other items in this scale concern parents' rejection or acceptance of their children's behavior and feelings, aggressiveness, need for affection, and self-expression. The fourth scale, *Understanding*, is heavily weighted with items dealing with communication between parents and children—including freedom of expression, talking out problems, and joint participation in decision-making. The parent at the upper end of this scale believes in the importance of sharing and communicating attitudes, feelings, and problems, while the parent at the lower end believes that "children should be seen and not heard."

The items that define *Trust*, the fifth scale, are mainly those which deny the individuality of the child. In these items, children are seen merely as extensions of the parent, not as individuals in their own right. Thus, the feeling is that they are not to be trusted, have to be watched, and must have even their innermost thoughts guarded. Conversely, parents who disagree with these items have enough respect for their children as individuals to feel that they can be trusted.

Since many persons have a tendency to form a response "set" to an Agree-Disagree type of item, two additional statements were used as buffers, or "set-breakers." The first two items in the final form of the Parent-Attitude Survey were "set-breakers," one a statement with which nearly all parents would agree, the other a statement with which nearly all would disagree. This precaution reduced the tendency of some subjects to begin, and then continue, marking the "Undecided" category for every item. These two items were not, however, scored as part of any of the attitude scales.

A Deviant Response scale was also construed as an internal check both on the subject's comprehension of the items and on the care with which he filled out the answer sheet. Of the 385 possible responses to the entire scale (77 items with 5 possible responses to each item), those 61 responses least frequently chosen by the standardization group were designated as "deviant" (in the sense of being infrequent). Each of these responses was extreme—that is, Strongly Agree or Strongly Disagree—and each was selected by less than 5 per cent of the standardization group. A subject's Deviant Response (DR) score was simply the number of his infrequent choices. A high score was taken to mean that the subject either did not understand the items or the instructions, or had been careless in marking his responses, and therefore the attitude-scale scores for that subject were probably not valid. A low score was considered evidence that the other scores did accurately reflect the subject's intentions. A DR score of 19 was used as the cutting point throughout the statistical analysis. Parent-Attitude Surveys with a DR score of 19 or above were not used.

Reliability and Intercorrelations of the Scales. The reliability of the five attitude scales was computed by means of the split-half method.[3] The reliability coefficients are presented in Table 6. These values are well within the satisfactory range of reliability for measuring instruments of this type.

Although the scales had been constructed to measure different areas of parent attitudes and the items had been sorted for their appropriateness to each area, the possibility still remained that all the scales might be measuring the same broad, undefined dimension of parent attitude. To investigate this possibility an interscale correlation matrix was computed in which every scale was correlated with every other scale.

A high correlation coefficient between two scales indicated that, to a

[3] Reliability is the precision or consistency with which a device measures a particular dimension or trait. Using the split-half method for estimating reliability, each scale was divided into two equal parts (the first 7 items in one part and the last 7 items in the other part), the middle item being omitted. Part scores were computed separately for each scale, using the 72 persons in the standardization group. The correlation between the two part-scores for each scale was determined, providing a reliability estimate when corrected for the length of the scale. Accordingly, a high correlation coefficient indicated that a scale was internally consistent in its measurement, and therefore reliable. A low coefficient showed just the opposite.

TABLE 6

Interscale Correlations of the Parent-Attitude Survey
(72 Subjects)

Scale	Scale 2	3	4	5	Mean r[1]	Split-half Reliability
1. Confidence	.36	.33	.34	.38	.36	.78
2. Causation		.57	.35	.53	.46	.77
3. Acceptance			.48	.62	.51	.68
4. Understanding				.61	.45	.86
5. Trust					.54	.84
		Mean Interscale Correlation			.46	.80

[1] Averages of correlations were computed by z-transformation-of-r prior to summation.

great extent, they measured the same attitude; a low coefficient showed that the two scales were relatively discrete, or measured different attitudes. The intercorrelations obtained were all positive, ranging from .33 to .62, a result that might be expected for scales measuring content in the same broad area. The correlation coefficients were high enough to indicate that all the scales were measuring related parent attitudes, but not so high as to suggest duplication.

PARENT-INTERVIEW SCHEDULE[4]

Development of the Interview Schedule. Each prospective subject in every research group was sent a letter explaining the purpose of the requested interview. Later he was asked by telephone for an appointment, and the appointment was arranged at his convenience, within the limitation that the interview must be conducted before the discussion series began. The interview was conducted in the home of the parent by interviewers hired and trained for this purpose.[5]

[4] The final form of the interview schedule, including relevant material, appears in Appendix A.

[5] Most of the interviewers were housewives, although some were teachers, school counselors, and nurses. A total of 44 interviewers participated, although by far the majority of the interviews were taken by only 15 individuals. With the exceptions of assigning Negro interviewers to Negro subjects, Spanish-speaking interviewers to Latin-American subjects, and (usually) male interviewers to fathers, the assignment of interviewer to subject was at random. Each interviewer worked with subjects from different schools, different research groups, and did both initial and final interviews.

Before asking the parent questions about his attitudes and behavior in his relations with his child, the interviewer obtained answers to questions for an Identification Sheet. This information gave the sex, age, and school grade of the parent's children; the age and amount of education of both parents; occupation of the principal wage earner; religious affiliation and frequency of church attendance.

The questions which the parent was then asked to answer were of a structured type. The following seven areas of parental attitudes and behavior, selected on the basis of their relevance for the hypotheses of the study, were therefore covered by fairly broad questions, followed by specific probes:

Difficulties in Child Rearing

"*All parents have some difficulties in raising children. In general, what has been the hardest thing about child rearing for you?*" This lead question was followed by probes concerning what caused the parent's difficulties, what he did about them, whether they were common or unusual, and where he turned for help with these problems.

What Parents Like about Parenthood

"*A parent is expected to do many things—and make many decisions—as a part of the job of raising children. Some of the things are fun, some are not so much fun. As you think about it, what are the things that please you most about being a parent?*" This second question was followed by a probe concerning the way in which the subject felt most effective as a parent, and how he accounted for this effectiveness.

Parental Worries

"*What are the things that worry you most about being a parent?*" Probes in the third area included questions about the causes of parental worries and the areas in which the parent felt most ineffective as a parent.

Amount of Freedom Given Child

"*Sometimes it's hard to know just where to draw the line with children. How much freedom do you allow your children?*" Probes following this question included a request for examples to illustrate the answer, a query as to how the parent's strictness or leniency compared with that of other families in the neighborhood, and a specific question as to whether or not the parent had restrictions about whom his own child should play with.

Punishment

"*Sometimes it is necessary to punish a child. What method of punishment do you usually use?*" This question was followed by probes about what the child was punished for, the effectiveness of punishment, and how often punishment was necessary.

Family Troubles

"*Most all families have trouble getting along from time to time. Where does the trouble usually occur in your family?*" Follow-up questions here included the persons usually involved and the situations in which trouble was likely to develop. The parent was also asked whether there was anyone unrelated to the family who regularly took care of the children, and whether this arrangement caused any problems.

Ideal Child, Ideal Parent

"*None of us is perfect, of course, and neither are our children. But what do you consider to be the ideal characteristics of an elementary-school age child?*" Probes concerning specific areas, such as behavior, getting along with others, and relations with parents, followed this general question. Finally, the subject was asked what he considered the most important characteristics of a good parent.

To obtain more precise socioeconomic data, the interviewer filled out, at the time of the interview and on the basis of his own observations, a rating sheet concerning the neighborhood and the home of the subject. (The subject was not asked for this information.) The neighborhood rating included such items as type of neighborhood, traffic density, spacing of dwelling units, play space for children, and the general condition of the neighborhood. The home rating included the type of house, amount of living space, the condition of the house, and a comparison of it with other homes in the neighborhood.

After the initial period of use the interview schedule was revised slightly (as shown in Appendix A) to eliminate questions which had proved unproductive.

Coding of the Interview Data. The responses of parents to the interview questions were tabulated according to a content code developed empirically by means of a content analysis of the responses of a representative sample of 46 interviews. Answers to each of the 28 questions in the interview were typed individually on cards and classified according to content. Each group of similar responses was assigned a code number. For example, all 46 responses to the question concerning what parents punished their children for were listed together. Then all the responses that gave disobedience as a reason for punishment were grouped and assigned the code-number 1. Every response listing unfairness as a cause for punishment was given the code-number 2, each listing untruthfulness was given the number 3, and so on, until all 46 responses in the sample were coded. The number of response codes for the different questions varied from 2 to 24, depending on the complexity of the question. Once the coding system was established, the remainder of the interviews were coded by assigning to each response the code number appropriate to its content. When a response was not covered by the code, or gave insufficient information, a code of zero was used. (The complete interview code is presented in Appendix A.)

The code numbers for each interview were first entered on data sheets and then transferred to IBM punched cards for greater ease in mass-data processing. The coding of all the interviews was done by eight graduate students from the Departments of Education, Sociology, and Psychology at the University of Texas. After receiving their instructions (see Appendix A) these students then worked independently of the Project staff in order to insure impartiality in the coding. The order of the interviews was intermixed for coding, so that each coder received interviews from different schools, different research groups, and initial and final measurements. They had no knowledge of the hypotheses of the study, of the research category of the subjects, or of whether the interviews were taken before or after the educational program. Interjudge reliability of the coding method was determined by having three of the coders independently code each of 40 interviews selected at random from the total sample. Among all three coders the percentage of complete agreement on the 28 items ranged from 63 to 100 per cent, with a mean of 78 per cent. The percentage of complete disagreement among all three coders ranged from zero to 12 per cent, with a mean of 2.5 per cent. This level of interjudge reliability, while not perfect, was as good as or better than that usually obtained for content coding and was considered to be satisfactory for use with large groups.

RESEARCH ON CHILDREN

SOCIOMETRIC EVALUATION OF CHILDREN

The Sociometric Method. We found it necessary to devise a method by which we could measure the individual elementary-school child's acceptability to his classmates. The usual sociometric techniques were inadequate for our purpose because their distribution of choices is always badly skewed; that is, a few of the children receive nearly all the choices and many of the children receive none. Furthermore, since the results of most sociometric methods are presented pictorially, in the form of a sociogram, the comparison of results for children from different groups is impossible.

The method adopted for our Project provided a numerical score for each child and a reasonably normal distribution of scores for each class. This technique made it possible to compute a standard score for each child which could, in turn, be compared to those of children from other classes. Moreover, the method offered many other less tangible but equally desirable advantages: it elicited a high motivational level on the part of the children, provided protection from embarrassment to those children not chosen, was applicable to grades one through six, and required only fifteen or twenty minutes of class time.

The sociometric method was based on having the child choose classmates to be on his "team," with each team sharing a prize at the end of the choosing. After being introduced by the teacher, a Project staff member would say to the class:

> We're going to have some fun today. First, we're going to divide the class into three teams, and each team will wear hats of a particular color. There'll be a red team, a white team, and a blue team. [At this point he brought out the colored hats.] After we've divided the class into three teams, we're going to let each of *you* choose whom you want to be on your team with you. When we're all through, each team will have a prize to share!" [At this point three satin bags, one red, one white, and one blue, were displayed.] But first, so we can keep track of you, we're going to give you some numbers to wear.

Each child was given a large numbered plaque to wear around his neck. He was also given one of the hats, so distributed that the class would be equally divided into thirds. Next the "team leader" (a Project staff member) instructed the children to line up in such a way that each child could see all the children on the other two teams. (This arrangement is illustrated in Fig. 5)

The children were then told that each was to choose by number two children from each of the other two teams—a total of four choices—and to write down their choices on a card provided for this purpose. After the children had made their choices the team leaders collected the cards and met in the middle of the room. A pretense was made of tallying the cards to see who would move to which team, though actually this period was used to check the legibility of the numbers and to see whether each child had made the correct number of choices. When the "tallying" was completed, two-thirds of the children on each team were rotated to the other two teams. For example, one-third of the children originally on the white

FIGURE 5

The Sociometric Method in Progress

team were moved to the blue team, another third was moved to the red team, and one-third remained on the white team. As a child moved to a different team he was given a different colored hat to wear. Although the children thought these changes were made on the basis of their choices, the changes were actually made according to a prearranged schedule of numbers.

When the first rotation was completed, the children were told that this method didn't always work so well the first time, that perhaps they didn't get to be on the team they wanted to be on, or maybe didn't get someone they wanted on their team. This was, of course, almost certain to be the situation, and the children wholeheartedly agreed that this was true. They were then told that they would be permitted to choose again, in the same manner as previously—two choices from each of the other two teams. Cards on which to write their choices were again distributed and the original procedure was repeated. When the second rotation was completed, the children were told that they would be permitted to make yet a third set of choices. Since every child was thus allowed to choose four teammates each time, the total number of choices per child was, of course, 12.

The prearranged schedule of numbers was such that every child had the opportunity to choose every other child. This arrangement also had the advantage of making every child think that he had been chosen in two of the three choosings. Therefore no child felt left out or unwanted by his classmates.

After the final rotation of children to the different teams, a prize bag was given to each team. The bags contained small individual prizes, such as pencils, erasers, rulers, or small pads with the name of the school printed on them. As soon as the prizes had been distributed, the number plaques and hats were collected, and the children returned to their seats. While these activities were going on, the teacher completed an Identification Sheet, listing the name of each child beside the number he had been wearing.

This sociometric method proved highly acceptable to both the children and the teachers. Word that members of the Project staff had arrived at a school passed around very quickly, and when they came to a classroom to play "the hat game" (as it came to be called) they were usually greeted with shouts of joy. Of some twelve thousand elementary-school children with whom this technique was used, only three refused to cooperate. One of these was a fifth-grade boy who went through the motions but refused to write down choices on his card. The other two were first-grade girls, one of whom was at school for the first time and appeared to be terrified by the entire situation; the other one refused at first but joined in as soon as the activity started.

The motivation of the children was quite high because—and this is another way in which our method differs from traditional sociometric methods—they thought that their choices were being acted upon immediately. This is quite different from asking a child whom he would like to take home to dinner when he knows very well that he is not really going to take anyone home to dinner. From comments made by the children during the choosing period it was apparent that they were making their choices on the basis of friendship and social acceptability, for they knew of no other reason to choose other children to be on their teams. When they asked on what basis they should make their choice, they were told to "choose a child with whom you would like to share a prize." To their questions about why they were doing this, we replied that we were doing some research to find out whom they would choose. It was occasionally necessary to break up small groups of collaborators, and to insist that each child make his own choices without being influenced by anyone else on his team. And a few times we had to prevent a child from trying to "beat the system" by signaling his friends not to choose him, so that he could remain on the same team and be with the friends he had chosen when the rotations were made. The small deception of using a prearranged schedule for rotation rather than the actual choices went undetected by the children during the entire four years of experimentation.

Since the directions were easy to understand and follow, and since the attention and motivation of the children was high, the administration of this sociometric device was not difficult. The only problems were with the first grade, where some of the children were unable to recognize or write the numbers and consequently required assistance from the staff. The teachers were usually quite interested in the method and were very cooperative. They were given the results both of the initial measurements and of the final measurements after all the evaluations had been completed. Reports from many of them indicated that they found this information quite useful.

Statistical Characteristics. The average test-retest reliabilities for the first three schools in which the method was used are presented in Table 7. The lower reliabilities in the first grade were probably due to the greater instability of the social structure at that level and to the difficulty some children had with recognizing and writing down the numbers. In general, however, these reliabilities were considered to be quite satisfactory for the measurement of such a nonspecific factor as social acceptability.

A small but insignificant difference based on sex was noted in the number of votes received: the means of the number of votes received by girls were slightly higher than the means of those received by boys. When the data were tabulated according to the four possibilities of choice by sex—boy choosing boy, boy choosing girl, girl choosing girl, and girl choosing boy—the sex differences were quite marked, significant beyond the .01 level of confidence in all classes. This difference was in the direction of same-sex choices; boys usually chose other boys, and girls usually chose other girls.[6]

TABLE 7

Test-Retest Reliability of the Sociometric Evaluation by Grade Level

Grade	No. of Classes	Mean Reliability[1]
1	7	.47
2	7	.68
2–3	2	.68
3	6	.80
4	7	.60
5	4	.61
5–6	4	.80
6	4	.74

[1] To compute means, z-transformation-of-r was used.

[6] A similar tabulation was made in one school using Latin-American versus Anglo-American children instead of sex differences. In this case the four possibilities were, of course, Latin choosing Latin, Latin choosing Anglo, Anglo choosing Anglo, and Anglo choosing Latin. The differences among the four possibilities were small and not of statistical significance, although these results should be interpreted in light of the fact that only 14 per cent of the children in this school were of Latin-American origin.

The frequency distribution of the raw scores (the actual number of choices received by each child) approached normality in all the classes, although one end of the distribution usually tended to be slightly truncated owing to the fact that it was impossible to receive fewer than zero number of choices. The mean number of choices for each class was automatically 12, since each child made 12 choices. The possible range of choices received was from zero to twice the number of children in the class (a child could conceivably receive two-thirds of the class votes in each of the three choosings). In actual practice there was usually one child, occasionally two, who received no choices. At the other end of the distribution, it was quite unusual for a child to receive more than half the total number of choices possible.

The raw scores were transformed to standard scores having a mean of zero and a standard deviation of 1, thus permitting a uniform comparison of the sociometric standing of children from different classes and schools, a comparison essential for the research design. The standard scores ranged from about −3 at the low end of the distribution to about +4 at the upper end, depending on the amount of deviation from the average. A child with a raw score of 12 (exactly at the mean) received a standard score of zero.

TEACHER RATINGS OF CHILDREN

These ratings consisted of the teacher's evaluation of the over-all adjustment of the child to the classroom setting. For purposes of the rating, the following components of "adjustment" were included in the information issued to the teachers.

Adjustment to the Classroom Setting[7]

The particular factors to keep in mind concerning classroom adjustment are:

The child's relation with you, the teacher.
How well he is accepted by the other children.

[7] Originally the teachers had been asked to rate the children on three separate dimensions. In addition to over-all adjustment to the classroom setting, they had been asked to rate the child also in terms of the adequacy of his perception of himself and of his acceptability to his classmates. However, the intercorrelations of these three ratings demonstrated that, in spite of the explanations of the various dimensions, the teachers were actually making their judgments on all three ratings in terms of adjustment. For this reason, the two latter ratings were eliminated.

His reaction to rules and regulations.
His attitude and cooperativeness.
His general emotional maturity.

This Project is *not* directly interested in the child's academic achievement or his intelligence level. Neither is the research concerned with the social or economic status of his family, nor the kind of adjustment problem a child may have. For example, a very withdrawn child and a very aggressive child might both receive the same low ranking.

The teachers made the judgments by placing each child in one of nine ranges of adjustment, through the medium of a forced, normalized distribution. Each teacher was provided with a stack of small cards on each of which had been typed the name of a child in the class; the names were given as they appeared on the roster prepared for sociometric identification. These the teacher sorted into nine piles, ranging from best adjustment to poorest adjustment. The number of cards to go into each pile had been predetermined in order to yield a normal distribution for each classroom. A rating of 1 indicated the best adjustment—9, the poorest. Each pile of cards was placed in an envelope and returned to the Project staff for tallying. The teachers did this task at their own convenience, and most of them reported that it required from fifteen to twenty minutes. (Complete instructions for the teacher rating are reproduced in Appendix A.)

In one school we were able to compute interjudge reliabilities, as three teachers and the principal took turns in instructing the same fifth-grade class. The interjudge reliabilities (correlation coefficients) in this situation ranged from .81 to .94. The fact that the test-retest reliabilities for the teacher ratings proved to be equally high was somewhat disadvantageous for measuring change. It seems highly unlikely that the incidence of change would be so small, hence the reasons for these high reliabilities are not clear. Perhaps many of the teachers, all of whom were unaware of the purpose of the measurements, may have assumed that the aim of the investigation was to ascertain the consistency of teacher judgments, and for this reason showed fewer changes in their ratings of children than the facts warranted. Or perhaps three months is too short a period for most teachers to change their first impression of the over-all adjustment of a child to the classroom setting.

Another disadvantage of this teacher-rating method was the lack of assurance that all the teachers used the same frame of reference in measuring adjustment, even though what we wished them to consider as adjustment to the classroom setting had been made clear in the instructions issued to them.[8]

The teacher-rating method met with reasonable success as far as its administration was concerned. Only two teachers failed to complete the ratings for their class. Many teachers, however, expressed dissatisfaction with the forced distribution, as they were reluctant to assign the lower ratings to any of the children in their classes.

[8] An attempt had been made earlier to modify the teacher-rating method so that it would provide behavioral classifications instead of judgments. Research was conducted to ascertain typical categories of behavioral descriptions of children, in order that the teachers could then classify the behavioral characteristics of the children in their classes according to these categories. Toward this aim, about 200 such descriptions were collected from elementary-school teachers attending a summer session at the University of Texas. This material was transferred to cards and sorted for comparability, in the hope that from six to ten reasonably discrete behavioral descriptions would emerge. Unfortunately, this was not the case. Only three typical behavioral descriptions were derived by this method, and these three were based primarily on adjustment to classroom setting. Since three categories were not enough for the purposes of our Project, the experiment was considered unsuccessful and was discontinued.

VII

Conducting the Research

THE PROBLEMS OF EVALUATIVE RESEARCH ON A PROGRAM in progress in a community, let it be said again, are quite different from those encountered in a laboratory, university, clinic, or hospital. Certainly control of subjects is far less possible. They are more difficult to locate and to study; and, much more than in other settings, the researcher is dependent on the good will of his subjects and of the community at large. Furthermore, the concept of community research does not enjoy the consistently high status or meet with the ready acceptance usually accorded that in laboratories or institutions. The conductor of community research is likely to meet with apathy at best; suspicion and hostility at worst. Hence just the mere mechanics of carrying out research in the community setting can present problems as uniquely challenging as those encountered in the actual research design and measurement construction themselves.

PRELIMINARY PROCEDURES

The first step toward collecting data was to establish a mutually satisfactory working agreement with the school administration, for obtaining the sociometric measurements and teacher ratings would require time from class and teacher, and the parents-subjects would have to be reached through the schools. After carefully studying the measuring instruments and methods of procedure, the Superintendent of Schools, Irby Carruth, granted permission for the Project to conduct its research in the Austin schools. He did not give the program the endorsement or official support of the public-school system. The decision of whether or not to cooperate with the Research Project was left to the individual principals and teachers, and the school administration exerted no influence on them, insisting also that the participation of parents be entirely voluntary, and that no pressure or even implication of pressure to cooperate be exerted upon them. The fact that the research was not a part of the school's program or activities likewise had to be made clear to parents. Thus the policy of completely voluntary participation was established and scrupulously observed throughout the course of the Project. Parents who did not want to be interviewed were not urged or pressured, and interviewers were instructed to terminate any interview if the parent became resistive. The same policy was followed in regard to principals and teachers, who understood that their cooperation was strictly voluntary.

Since the discussion-group portion of the educational program was organized through the PTA, the school principal usually not only was aware that the program was to take place, but often was actively involved in organizing it. Although he was given complete information as to what the research proposed to do, the PTA representatives were not, for the research and educational activities were to be kept separate as much as possible to prevent their influencing each other in any way. This separation was, in general, successful. The parents and the PTA organizers knew that the interviews were going on, but were generally unaware that the purpose of the research was to evaluate the educational program specifically. Indeed, most parents showed little curiosity about the goals of the research. The explanation that the study concerned parent-child relations was usually all the parent wanted to know. It was never denied that the research was to enable us to evaluate the educational method, but the relationship between the research and the educational program was neither explained nor publicized in general.

We received good cooperation from the school principals. Many of them were quite interested in the research and went out of their way to be helpful. Others were less interested but still agreeable to having the research conducted in their schools. In only two or three cases was a principal either reluctant to give permission or grudging in his cooperation, and in only one instance was there an outright refusal. In all cases, however, the principals required a thorough explanation of the goals and purposes of the research as well as a detailed description of the proposed activities with children, teachers, and parents. The justifiability of using class time to collect the sociometric data was questioned by only three principals, all principals of Negro schools. No consistent objection arose in regard to the program. Most principals felt that the time required from the pupils and teachers would be adequately offset by having the results of the sociometric measurements made available to the teacher after the final testing.

COLLECTING THE DATA

The collecting of data in the schools proceeded with reasonable smoothness, the main problem being that of scheduling. Fortunately, by allowing a week or more between the opening meetings of the various discussion groups it was possible to space the research workload so that a relatively small staff could collect the large amount of data required. Since all the initial measurements on all groups had to be completed before the discussion program began, this scheduling sometimes went awry; on three occasions, discussion groups met without the accompanying research having been done.

The sociometric device worked very well in the actual application. Pupils and teachers alike found it highly acceptable since it provided a break in the day's routine, was intrinsically interesting, afforded an opportunity for some physical movement around the room, and gave each student a small "prize." An early decision to use the device only in classrooms where there were children whose parents were in one of the research groups was quickly and happily reversed because, once the students knew about the "hat game," none of them wanted to be left out. The main disadvantage of this device, from the viewpoint of collecting data, was student absences. Owing to the purpose of the research, it was essential that each child be present on the days of both the initial and the final measurements; data lost by absence could not be recovered.

The data from the teacher ratings were also relatively easy to obtain. The packets of material were distributed and collected by the school secretary who, in most cases, simply placed them in the teachers' boxes at school. The teacher-rating device was self-administering, and required only about fifteen minutes. Reminders to complete the ratings were sometimes necessary, but, as mentioned earlier, in the entire course of the Project, only two teachers failed to return the ratings.

Obtaining data from parents was much more difficult. The interview and the attitude scales, requiring from an hour to two hours to complete, were administered individually in the parent's home by an interviewer especially trained for this purpose. The first contact was made by mail with the parent, whose name and address were obtained from the registration card for all groups except the Random-Control Group; these we obtained from the school files. Just how to phrase the letter, which explained briefly the purpose of the interview and requested an appointment to be arranged by telephone, was a delicate problem throughout the Project. The request for an interview, no matter how carefully worded as to our interests and as to the voluntary aspect of the parent's cooperation, seemed to trigger any anxiety the parent might have in relation to his children or to his role as a parent. Not a single untoward reaction resulted from the interview itself, but the *request* for an interview made many parents feel uncomfortable.

The apprehensions aroused by the letter might have been partially avoided by sending it out over the principal's signature, a procedure which some principals suggested. This method was not adopted, however, because school sponsorship of the Project might then have been implied and pressure indirectly exerted on the parents to participate in the research. The first letters therefore went out under the letterhead of the Mental Health Association. But we soon discovered that the words "mental health" produced anxiety in many parents, so by far the bulk of the subsequent requests went under the letterhead of the "Parent-Child Relations Project" and bore the signature of the research director.

In spite of the fact that the letter carried the telephone number and specifically invited inquiries for additional information, only one parent called that number during the entire course of the Project. Parents actually made many calls concerning the interview request, but they directed their inquiries mainly to teachers, principals, or other parents. A few calls went to the central administration offices of the public school system and some to the Better Business Bureau. The interviewing aspect of the Project had already been cleared with the Better Business Bureau in anticipation of this reaction.

A call from a parent usually came to the attention of the principal of the school sooner or later. In almost every case, the parent merely wanted reassurance that the request for the interview had nothing to do with his child's achievement or behavior in school. In a few cases the letter also evoked more severe reactions in certain parents, such as the suspicion that they had been "turned in" by neighbors, or that the request was really a "cover-up" for an investigation by juvenile authorities. In a limited number of cases the principal felt that a parent was so emotionally disturbed that any inquiry would be an upsetting experience, and consequently no further attempt was made to obtain an interview.

Arranging appointments for interviews was not an easy matter. At first, appointments were scheduled centrally in the office of the Project, but this method proved too cumbersome, and thereafter most of the appointments were scheduled by the interviewers themselves. In the lower socioeconomic areas this scheduling was further complicated by the fact that some of the parents did not have telephones. The rejection rate for the request for an appointment was about 15 per cent, the usual reason given by the subjects being lack of time. This percentage of refusal was approximately the same in the various research groups and in the different geographic regions of the city. Obtaining interviews with fathers was particularly difficult. Working mothers also were reluctant to give up an hour or two of their free time. For these reasons, many of the interviews had to be conducted in the evening, after working hours. When both the father and the mother were included in a research group, the best results were obtained when two interviewers shared the appointment, for the parents could then be interviewed simultaneously.

Difficulties were also encountered in interviewing the two ethnic minorities in Austin. In the case of the Negro parents the basic matter of finding them constituted a major problem. In fact, it proved practically impossible for an Anglo interviewer to locate a Negro parent, for, acting on the assumption that the stranger was a bill collector or a bearer of other bad tidings, the subject's neighbors and sometimes his own family would give misinformation concerning his whereabouts. After a number of unsuccessful attempts to secure the interviewers, the Project revised its tactics and used Negro interviewers exclusively for this phase of the research. These interviewers[1] met with none of the obstacles encountered

[1] Four graduate students from the Department of Sociology of Huston-Tillotson College, Austin, Texas.

by their predecessors, and probably were better able to establish rapport with the subjects than Anglo interviewers would have been. In the case of the Latin-American parents the main problem was that of language. Many of these parents spoke no English, and others spoke English which was not adequate for interviewing purposes. This barrier was removed by using bilingual interviewers of Latin-American descent.

Many appointments were broken and frequently parents failed to be home at the appointed time. Hence a great deal of persistence on the part of the interviewer was necessary to obtain the data even from those subjects who were willing to cooperate. Efforts were further hampered in one school district by a group of encyclopedia salesmen operating under the name of "Parent-Child Study Survey." This group ostensibly was conducting a "scientific survey" but in reality was using this approach to gain entrance to homes in order to present a high-pressure sales campaign. Although the similarity in names was apparently accidental, the salesmen were quick to capitalize on the letters that the Project had sent out in this district. Therefore many parents and even the Better Business Bureau at first confused the salesmen with our legitimate interviewers who thus met many, and often indignant, refusals to cooperate. This unhappy situation was resolved by the Better Business Bureau, acting through the home office of the publisher of the encyclopedia.

The request for a second interview, to obtain final data, was no better received than the first one. Once more there was about a 15-per-cent refusal rate, and again primarily on the original basis of the subject's unwillingness to give the time required. On the other hand, parents evinced no anxiety or uncertainty regarding the purpose or nature of the second interview, as the experience with the first interview had apparently been reassuring to all of them. Neither were there any objections to the content of the interview or to the attitude scales, nor to the methods of interviewing or to the behavior of the interviewer. The major objection of the parents was always the same: *the time required.*

Moreover, parents who refused to give the second interview obviously did so with the feeling that participation in one interview was enough. They felt they had done their share. This attitude existed in spite of the fact that, at the time of the first interview, the parent had been forewarned that a second interview would be necessary in about three months. Practically all parents had originally agreed to this plan, but when the time for the second interview actually came their reaction was different. These refusals to cooperate in the final measurements were especially damaging to the evaluative research, as the investment in the initial measurements had already been made and no substitution of subjects was now possible. The explanation of this situation had little effect on the reluctant parent, however; he usually insisted that "it's someone else's turn now."

Even though these particular difficulties were encountered in collecting the interview data throughout the duration of the Project, no problems at all arose in the majority of cases. Most parents accepted the letter at face value, made and kept their appointment with the interviewer willingly, and raised no objection to the time required for the second interview. Many parents were not only willing to cooperate but were also interested in the procedure and pleased to be able to contribute. The parents received no reward of any kind. The time they gave was indeed an unselfish contribution to research.

Collecting the data on attendance and participation in the discussion groups was likewise a complex matter. Early in the Project we attempted to use a tape recorder in the discussion groups, but this proved unsatisfactory. It was impossible to obtain an intelligible recording because of differences in volume of the speakers' voices, the varying distances of the subjects from the recorder, the sounds of more than one person talking at the time, and such extraneous noises as shuffling feet and chairs being moved. Therefore we found it necessary to have an observer at every meeting to keep the pertinent records. Yet at the same time the natural structure or spontaneity of the group had to be preserved, so in order to give the observer a functional role, he was assigned the duty of operating the motion-picture projector. Since finding someone to operate the projector at a meeting is usually a problem, this solution was doubly advantageous. The observer thereby became an integral part of the group, and the group in turn had no reason to regard his presence as "foreign."

The question of who should be the observer and keep the records on attendance and participation was less easily resolved. Early experience had shown that anyone who could be even remotely regarded as a professional or specialist would be put in the "expert" role by the group. Thus a graduate student who was sent out as an observer became, unwillingly, the group's consultant; queries were referred to him, and his opinion was solicited. In brief, his presence altered the nature of the group considerably. The same difficulty was encountered when staff members of the Project were present, for they, too, either were viewed as a foreign element or were forced into the role of "experts" by the group.

Eventually the observers, who were usually parents themselves, were recruited from several sources. Some were friends of the Project staff and others were Project secretaries—all of them selected for their ability to merge with the group. Hiring observers seemed inadvisable, since the discussion leaders with whom they were to work would be contributing their time on a volunteer basis. The most satisfactory arrangement, therefore, and the one under which the bulk of the attendance and participation data was collected, was to use inexperienced group-discussion leaders as observers. These prospective leaders had completed their training in the discussion-leaders' workshop but had not yet led a group of their own. They usually welcomed the opportunity to watch an experienced leader in action and felt that operating the projector and keeping the records was a small price to pay for the experience. This arrangement had the considerable additional benefits of seasoning new discussion leaders and of training leaders to operate motion-picture projectors. By virtue of their training and interest in group discussion these neophyte leaders fitted into the groups quite easily. Their presence was probably less disruptive than that of any other observers who might have been employed. The observer was not prohibited from participating in the discussion, as this limitation would have presented an awkward situation and served to emphasize his special status. Neither did the observer make a secret of keeping the records. He usually took his place in the circle with the other group members, and their questions regarding his record keeping received the vague but courteous answer that he was trying to find out something about discussion-group procedure. Actually, most of the observers had little more information to give. As the observers had a genuine reason for being present and were accepted as group members, the curiosity that might otherwise have been expected concerning their record keeping was greatly reduced.

One disadvantage in using prospective leaders for observers was that their interest and commitment were directed toward discussion leadership rather than toward research activities. Although the resulting attendance records[2] probably have a satisfactory degree of accuracy, since one of the first duties of a discussion leader was to help everyone learn everyone else's name, the probable accuracy of the records on participation and personal reference may be quite a different matter. Even when a discussion moves rapidly this kind of tallying of verbal participation need not be difficult, but it requires a fairly high degree of attention on the part of the observer. Since our observers were present mainly out of interest in leading discussions and not in keeping records, their attention to the latter was not always consistently sustained. For our purposes, it seemed better to sacrifice some accuracy in the records than to risk disturbing the harmony of the group; hence the data obtained in this manner we consider as yielding only approximate measures of the degree of personal involvement.

THE RESEARCH POPULATION

Data on the number of cases in the various groups constituting the research population are summarized in Table 8. These cases were obtained in the course of seven research periods, corresponding approximately to a school semester, from 1956 through 1960. The small percentage of fathers represented here is due to two factors: fathers were usually more reluctant to be interviewed than mothers; and not as many fathers were asked to participate as mothers. The ratio of fathers to mothers was determined by the registration for the discussion program. When both father and mother registered, an attempt was made to interview both, and to obtain a counterbalancing couple in the control groups. Since fewer fathers than mothers attended the discussion groups, proportionately fewer fathers were in all the research categories. In no instance was a parent included in the Experimental Group unless he actually attended the discussion program.

Data-collection procedures were complicated by the necessity of gearing the research activities to the educational program which was, in turn, dependent on the cooperation and schedules of other groups not at all concerned with the research. The high attrition rate that is usually a concomitant of research on "noncaptive" groups was made even higher

[2] These attendance records were also necessary for the PTA in awarding the certificates at the completion of the study session.

TABLE 8

The Research Population

Research Group	No. of Cases	Parents: Fathers (by Percentage)	Parents: Mothers (by Percentage)	No. of Cases	Children: Boys (by Percentage)	Children: Girls (by Percentage)
Initial Measurements Only						
Experimental	453	15.9	84.1	547	51.6	48.4
Lecture-Control	143	16.9	83.1	167	52.1	47.9
Nonattendant-Control	199	14.6	85.4	233	49.8	50.2
Random-Control	364	15.1	84.9	436	48.8	51.2
All groups	1,159	15.4	84.6	1,383	50.5	49.5
Initial Measurements and Final Measurements						
Experimental	370	14.6	85.4	434	51.2	48.8
Lecture-Control	102	15.7	84.3	116	51.7	48.3
Nonattendant-Control	160	13.8	86.2	204	50.0	50.0
Random-Control	271	13.3	86.7	333	49.2	50.8
All groups	903[1]	14.2	85.8	1,087	50.4	49.6

[1] These totals represent individual parents or children, not families, for in some cases, both parents or more than one child in a single family are included. Initial measurements were completed on 981 families and complete data were obtained on 775 families. Only children enrolled in elementary school were included in the research sample.

in this instance by our absolute dependence on voluntary cooperation by the subjects. Since the nature of the research design made the replacement of "lost" subjects impossible, the attrition rate was especially damaging.

Although we made every effort to secure a representative sample of elementary-school children and their parents in Austin, the attempt was only partially successful. As just mentioned, the sample included comparatively few fathers, a reflection of the tendency of fathers to participate less than mothers in parental education. With respect to the ethnic minorities, Negroes were represented in the sample in about the same proportion as in the population of Austin, whereas Latin Americans were not adequately represented because of the relatively greater difficulty in recruiting Latin-American discussion leaders and in organizing discussion groups at schools in predominately Latin-American districts. With regard to the other major variables—social class, education, occupation, and age—the sample was a fair representation of elementary-school children and their parents in Austin.

The question of possible bias in the sample due to measuring techniques is a difficult one to answer. This problem did not enter into the measurements with children, since teacher ratings were obtained on virtually all subjects and since the sociometric measurements were affected only by absences from school. While absences may have exerted a biasing influence on the sample (e.g., sickly children are more likely to be absent, thus the sample is not representative on the variable of sickliness), their influence seems to have been inconsequential. The problem of bias in the parent data is a more serious one, however, since the parent had the option of declining to participate. Is the parent who refuses to be interviewed different in some important respect from the parent who agrees? No answer to this question exists, since his refusal makes it impossible to study the uncooperative parent and to learn what he is like. While the actual basis for the refusal cannot be determined, the stated reason in almost every case was lack of time. In this respect the parents who refused were not necessarily different from the others, for loss of the time required for the interview was also a consistent complaint of those who cooperated.

While we made no attempt to obtain a sample representative of the population of elementary-school children and their parents in the United States, a description of Austin might make it easier to compare it with cities in other parts of the country. Austin is a city of 185,000 people, the capital of the state, and the site of the University of Texas, with nearly 21,500 students (1962). For a city of its size, it has relatively little light industry and no heavy industry at all. While Austin does serve the surrounding agricultural area to some extent, the city is not a transportation or shipping center. In addition to housing the extensive governmental offices, it serves as the headquarters or home office for many state-wide organizations of all kinds. Austin might therefore be described as a white-collar community in which the emphasis is on governmental and educational pursuits. As a result, the educational level of the general population is probably higher than average. The proportion of people in the middle class is greater and the proportion of those in the upper and lower classes is less than would be normally expected in a city of this size. Austin is in about middle position, compared with the state as a whole, as far as ethnic minorities are concerned. The Negro population is not so heavy as in the eastern part of the state, but higher than that in the western part. Similarly, more Latin Americans are to be found in southern Texas and along the border than in Austin, and fewer in the northern part of the state. Legal segregation of Negroes at the elementary-school level existed in Austin at the time of this study. Latin Americans were not segregated, but in a few school districts the proportion of Latin Americans was 75 per cent or more.

The measurements used in this Project produced two major types of data. Quantified scores were derived from the Parent-Attitude Survey, the sociometric device, and the teacher ratings, while qualitative information was obtained from the parent interview. The quantitative data were evaluated through analysis of variance, factor analysis, and covariance analysis. The qualitative information was treated as frequency data and analyzed statistically by the use of the chi-square technique. In the different analyses the number of cases varied because of missing data of one kind or another, or, as in the case of the analysis of variance, because of the necessity of balancing the cell frequencies through random selection. In all the statistical treatments of the Parent-Attitude Survey the rare individual having a Deviant Response score of 19 or higher was removed, since such a high DR score would have cast serious doubt on the accuracy of the attitude scales for such persons.

An identifying code number for parents and children was used throughout the Project to insure their anonymity. All data were processed by means of the IBM punched-card system, and the calculations were performed on an IBM 650 Electronic Computer.[3]

[3] IBM equipment at the University of Texas was made available by the Computation Center, the Testing and Counseling Center, and the Department of Sociology.

VIII

Parental Attitudes and Behavior

"WHAT ARE THESE PARENTS LIKE?" NATURALLY WE ADdressed ourselves to this question with great interest when data on the parents were in hand.

To answer this basic question, it was imperative to have information concerning the subjects' problems, worries, ideas on parent-child relations, and interaction with their children. The instrument used to ascertain the attitudes and behavior of this group was the parent interview.

The data from the interviews are presented here not as scores but as frequencies representing how many (or what percentage) of the parents gave a particular response or answer to a certain question. By tabulating the responses of the entire research sample through use of the interview code (see Appendix A), tables were constructed for all the questions in the first interview. In this way an over-all picture of the attitudes and behavior of this group of parents was obtained before the educational method itself was introduced. These base-line data are presented in a modified form of bar graphs throughout this chapter. The numbers assigned to the questions in the original interview schedule have been retained in connection with the figures showing the bar graphs in order to aid the reader in correlating data in the text with the interview schedule reproduced in Appendix A. Consequently the numerical order of these questions had to be disregarded in incorporating them in the text.

In the figures the number of respondents varies, since the numbers do not include those who gave responses which fell in the "No Information" category and those whose answers could not be coded. Similarly, in questions such as Question 3, "Parental Worries," responses coded as "No Worries" are not included. The totals in the figures, therefore, vary greatly. The percentages represent subjects who responded, not all those who were asked. Some of the questions on the interview proved unproductive or uncodable and were therefore not used in the tabulations. Many of the questions were coded for both a first and second response, and, in one case, a third response. The frequency tables for the second response are not presented because, except for their greatly reduced number, they are very similar to those of the first response. Hence the following descriptions are based entirely on the parent's initial response to a question in the interview.

CHILD-REARING PROBLEMS AND SOLUTIONS

The first question on the interview dealt with difficulties in rearing children. Two major areas of concern—discipline of the child and problems within the parent—stood out in the responses (see Fig. 6). About one-third of the parents saw discipline as their greatest problem in child rearing. Responses in this area included such items as the child's not paying attention when spoken to, disobedience, or lack of cooperation (difficulty in making the child do something). Slightly more than one-fourth of the parents responded to the question with self-oriented problems (such as inadequacy, indecision, or inconsistency). The fact that only 7 per cent of the parents mentioned a specific symptom in the child —for example, thumbsucking, phobias, or wetting—indicated that the needs of this research population were of a normal rather than a clinical nature.

The follow-up probe then asked what the parent had done to solve the problem he described (see Fig. 7). The most frequent response (30 per cent) was that he had changed his own behavior or attitude. Parents were reluctant to try to change the behavior of the child as a means of solving their difficulties. In fact, nearly half of the total number of these parents attempted to solve their child-rearing problems without directly changing the child; they preferred, instead, either to manipulate the environment in some manner or to change their own behavior. Those parents who en-

FIGURE 6

Difficulties in Rearing Children

Question 1. ***"All parents have some difficulties in raising children. In general, what has been the hardest thing about child rearing for you?"***

Response	Respondents	Percentage (0 . . . 10 . . . 20 . . . 30 . . . 40 . . . 50 . . . 60 . . . 70)
Discipline	354	33
Problem within parent	277	26
Sibling rivalry	100	10
Normal adjustment or developmental problems	94	9
Specific symptoms	77	7
No problem	72	7
Financial problems	48	4
Physical health, safety	46	4
Total	1,068	

deavored to change the behavior of the child did so mainly by explanation or reasoning rather than by punishment or rewards.

Parents were about equally divided in their opinion concerning the effectiveness of their methods of meeting these difficulties (see Fig. 8). Slightly more than half the number felt that their response to the situation really improved matters; the others could see only minor improvements or no change at all.

On the other hand, no doubt seemed to exist in the minds of most parents as to the main source of trouble in the family. Later in the interview, when parents were asked where trouble usually originated in the family, more than half of them listed the behavior of the children (see Fig. 9). This was a difficult question for parents to answer, however; although only 6 per cent of the sample said they had no family troubles,

FIGURE 7

Parental Responses to Difficulties

Question 1-*a*. ***"What have you done to help this situation*** **[described in Question 1]?"**

Response	Respondents	Percentage (0 . . . 10 . . . 20 . . . 30 . . . 40 . . . 50 . . . 60 . . . 70)
Changed own behavior or attitude	262	30
Explanations, reasoning	216	24
Manipulated environment	139	16
Punishment	91	10
Sought outside help	83	9
Has done nothing	70	8
Rewards or inducements	23	3
Total	884	

FIGURE 8

Effectiveness of Parental Responses to Difficulties

Question 1-*b*. ***"How has this*** **[action described in Question 1-*a*]** ***worked out?"***

Response	Respondents	Percentage (0 . . . 10 . . . 20 . . . 30 . . . 40 . . . 50 . . . 60 . . . 70)
Improvement	361	43
Slight improvement	279	33
No change	111	13
Great improvement	79	10
Made matters worse	6	1
Total	836	

FIGURE 9

Cause of Family Troubles

Question 6. ***"Most all families have trouble getting along from time to time. Where does the trouble usually occur in your family?"***

Response	Respondents	Percentage (0...10...20...30...40...50...60...70)
Behavior of child or children	224	51
Parental disagreements	80	18
Getting ready to go out or do something	42	9
Differences in age of children	29	7
Finances	23	5
Lack of time	22	5
Reaching family agreement on activities	23	5
Total	443	

FIGURE 10

Persons Involved in Family Troubles

Question 6-a. ***"What members of the family are most often involved in (or cause) the trouble?"***

Response	Respondents	Percentage (0...10...20...30...40...50...60...70)
Child or children	249	52
Parents	156	33
Others	70	15
Total	475	

FIGURE 11

Cause of Difficulties in Child Rearing

Question 1-c. ***"What do you think caused this situation* [described in Question 1] *to develop?***

Response	Respondents	Percentage (0 . . . 10 . . . 20 . . . 30 . . . 40 . . . 50 . . . 60 . . . 70)
Parent's behavior or attitude	251	32
Inherent characteristic of children	151	19
Environmental situation	145	18
Age relation	127	16
Normal development "stages"	38	5
Physical or health	32	4
Culture, society	20	3
Inherited	20	3
Total	784	

FIGURE 12

Commonness of Difficulties

Question 1-*d*. ***"How common are situations like this* [as described in Question 1] with other parents and children you know?"**

Response	Respondents	Percentage (0 . . . 10 . . . 20 . . . 30 . . . 40 . . . 50 . . . 60 . . . 70)
Very common	378	45
Common or fairly common	253	29
Unusual, unique, special	88	10
Occasional	82	9
Present in all families	63	7
Total	864	

more than half of the total responses were in the "No Information" or uncodable category. Reasonably enough, since most parents felt that the behavior of the child was at the root of family troubles, most parents also said that the children were the ones most frequently involved in troubles (see Fig. 10).

The basic cause of child-rearing problems was multifaceted (see Fig. 11). Although the parents held their children responsible for starting trouble, they simultaneously blamed themselves for this situation. Nearly one-third of the group felt their own behavior or attitude was the cause of their child-rearing difficulties. Other causes most frequently mentioned were the inherent (but not inherited) characteristics of the child, environmental situations, and age relations within the family.

When asked whether they felt that difficulties like their own were common in families, most of the parents indicated that their problems did not make them feel very "different" from others (see Fig. 12). Less than one-fifth of the parents felt that their problems were unusual or occurred only occasionally in other families. The remainder felt their difficulties were common or very common, a few (7 per cent) stating that they thought these were present in all families.

While many of the parents sought some form of outside help for solving the difficulties they described, a substantial number did not. Of all the parents interviewed, 47 per cent stated that they had not sought outside help with their child-rearing problems (see Fig. 13). When such help had been sought, the three major sources of assistance had been friends, physicians, and teachers. A somewhat striking finding was the infrequency with which these parents turned to their own families or relatives (only 5 per cent) for help with their child-rearing difficulties. Certainly parents in this sample did not "go home to mother" with their troubles—of 1,145 parents interviewed, only 6 said that they had sought help from their own mother on the matter.

Whatever source of outside help the parents used, they generally found it beneficial (see Fig. 14). Nearly three-fourths of the parents who had sought outside help evaluated the results positively, and only 11 per cent gave a completely negative appraisal.

FIGURE 13

Outside Help for Solving Problems

Question 1-e. ***"Have you ever sought outside help in this matter* [described in Question 1]?"**

Response	Respondents	Percentage (0 . . . 10 . . . 20 . . . 30 . . . 40 . . . 50 . . . 60 . . . 70)
Friend or neighbor	127	31
Physician	111	27
Teacher or school personnel	109	26
Professional agency	35	8
Member of family, relative	20	5
Individual specialist or practitioner other than physician	14	3
Total	416	

FIGURE 14

Effectiveness of Outside Help

Question 1-f. ***"How did this* [outside help] *work out?"***

Response	Respondents	Percentage (0 . . . 10 . . . 20 . . . 30 . . . 40 . . . 50 . . . 60 . . . 70)
Positive evaluation	278	72
Neutral evaluation	66	17
Negative evaluation	42	11
Total	386	

PARENTAL EFFECTIVENESS AND INEFFECTIVENESS

When subjects were asked in what ways they felt most effective as parents, 50 per cent specified providing for the child or taking care of him (see Fig. 15). Most of these responses were concerned with meeting the physical needs of children. The small percentage of subjects (10 per cent) who felt themselves effective in disciplining their children was consistent with the high frequency with which discipline was mentioned as a problem in the first question. Similarly, only a small number of parents (14 per cent) felt themselves most effective in offering companionship and sharing activities with their children.

Although, as shown through responses to an earlier question, these subjects did not turn to their own parents for help, they did attribute their parental effectiveness to what they had learned in their own childhood from their mothers and fathers (see Fig. 16); in fact, nearly half of the respondents said they learned from their own parents how to be effective with their children, while only 6 per cent named sources other than their parents, although many credited experience or parental interest as the

FIGURE 15

Parental Effectiveness

Question 2-a. ***"In what way do you feel that you are most effective as a parent?"***

Response	Respondents	Percentage (0...10...20...30...40...50...60...70)
Providing for or taking care of the child	478	50
Guidance, direction, teaching	247	26
Participation, sharing activities, companionship	139	14
Supervision, discipline, control	93	10
Total	957	

FIGURE 16

Reasons for Parental Effectiveness

Question 2-*b*. ***"How do you account for this [effectiveness]?"***

Response	Respondents	Percentage
Learned from own parents	291	42
Love, interest, parental feeling	252	36
Experience, practice	110	16
Learned from sources other than own parents	40	6
Total	693	

FIGURE 17

Parental Ineffectiveness

Question 3-*b*. ***"In what way do you feel most ineffective as a parent?"***

Response	Respondents	Percentage
Discipline	223	27
Lack of patience	214	26
Lack of time	124	15
Do not feel ineffective	84	10
Lack of knowledge	66	8
Inconsistency	52	6
Lack of closeness with child	51	6
Nervousness	18	2
Total	832	

source. Since the efforts of all media to educate parents for their parental role must be included in these "other sources," it seems clear that such efforts have not caused parents to feel more effective as parents.

Discipline and patience were mentioned most frequently as the areas in which parents felt least effective (see Fig. 17). On the other hand, lack of knowledge was given by only 8 per cent of them as the cause of their ineffectiveness, a percentage which further indicates that programs designed merely to give parents information on the parental role may indeed be missing the mark.

PLEASANT ASPECTS OF PARENTHOOD

Opinions concerning what parents like about parenthood were fairly well divided in this group (see Fig. 18). A third of the subjects enjoyed most the companionship and the love and affection which they received from their children. Almost a fourth of the group valued most the feel-

FIGURE 18

What Parents Like About Parenthood

Question 2. ***"A parent is expected to do many things—and make many decisions—as a part of the job of raising children. Some of these things are fun, some are not so much fun. As you think about it, what are the things that please you most about being a parent?"***

Response	Respondents	Percentage (0...10...20...30...40...50...60...70)
Companionship, receiving love and affection	355	33
Interesting, meaningful experience	266	25
Achievement by the child	248	23
Meeting the child's needs	145	14
Help or contribution by the child	59	5
Total	1,073	

ing of personal pride that they experienced because of their children's achievements. Another fourth felt that parenthood is of itself interesting and meaningful. Taking care of the child was not a source of primary satisfaction for these parents, although earlier many of them had said this was the area in which they felt themselves most effective. Only 14 per cent gave meeting the child's needs as an aspect of parenthood that they liked. Perhaps this percentage indicates that in American culture today parents may find that meeting a child's basic physical needs is too simple to be gratifying.

FIGURE 19

Parental Worries

Question 3. ***"What are the things that worry you most about being a parent?"***

Response	Respondents	Percentage (0 . . . 10 . . . 20 . . . 30 . . . 40 . . . 50 . . . 60 . . . 70)
Own adequacy	259	25
How child will turn out, character development	222	22
Physical: illness, accidents	195	19
Finances	98	9
Behavior and activity of child	65	6
Education, school grades	61	6
Specific problems or symptoms	51	5
Undesirable environmental situation	36	4
Separation, broken home	28	3
Religious or spiritual	14	1
Total	1,029	

PARENTAL WORRIES

Very few parents (3 per cent) stated that they had no worries. For a great many mothers and fathers (25 per cent) the most prevalent worry was their own adequacy as parents (see Fig. 19), an area which had already been given as the most frequent source of difficulties in child rearing. Almost as high a percentage of parents were primarily concerned about the future of the child, how he would "turn out." The only other worry mentioned with substantial frequency concerned the physical well-being of the child, a worry which existed even though physical considerations were not often mentioned as a problem on earlier questions and even though many parents felt most adequate in taking care of the physical needs of their children.

This triad of worries—self-adequacy, how the child will turn out, and concern for the physical safety of the child—seem to indicate that parenthood was actually an anxiety-producing role for this group.

PUNISHMENT: CAUSES FOR AND METHODS USED

Responses to earlier questions had indicated that parents were reluctant to resort to punishment as a means of solving their difficulties. Of the 1,145 parents interviewed, however, only seven said that they did not punish their children. By far the most common cause of punishment (see Fig. 20) was disobedience. Half of the parents listed this as the usual reason for punishing the child, and another 15 per cent gave insolence (which might well be considered a part of disobedience). The other frequently mentioned cause for punishment was aggressiveness. Only four parents of the total sample claimed that there was no need to punish their children.

As for method, corporal punishment was the type most frequently used (see Fig. 21); nearly half of the parents relied on this. The next most prevalent method was the withdrawal of privileges, followed closely by the use of confinement. Among the parents who used corporal punishment, spanking was the most common form.

The parents' evaluation of the effectiveness of their methods of punishment was clearly positive (see Fig. 22). When asked whether they thought their methods work, all but 5 per cent of the subjects responded that their method was effective, though 40 per cent of them qualified their statements in some way concerning the degree of the effectiveness.

FIGURE 20

Causes of Punishment

Question 5-b. *"What do you usually have to punish the child for?"*

Response	Respondents	Percentage (0...10...20...30...40...50...60...70)
Disobedience	539	50
Aggressiveness	207	19
Insolence	158	15
Carelessness	118	11
Untruthfulness	36	3
Unfairness, unkindness	19	2
Total	1,077	

FIGURE 21

Types of Punishment

Question 5. *"Sometimes it is necessary to punish a child. What method of punishment do you usually use?"*

Response	Respondents	Percentage (0...10...20...30...40...50...60...70)
Corporal punishment	519	46
Withdrawal of privileges	253	22
Confinement	221	20
Verbal	133	12
Total	1,126	

A question on the amount of freedom given the child (see Fig. 23) was also included in this area of parental control. The responses, ranging from very strict to lenient, were fairly evenly distributed. Discounting those parents who indicated that their practices varied with the situation, the majority felt that they gave their children more than the average amount

FIGURE 22

Effectiveness of Punishment

Question 5-c. ***"How do these methods [of punishment] work?"***

Response	Respondents	Percentage (0 . . . 10 . . . 20 . . . 30 . . . 40 . . . 50 . . . 60 . . . 70)
Effective or very effective	598	55
Effective (qualified)	439	40
Not effective	49	5
Total	1,086	

FIGURE 23

Amount of Freedom Given Child

Question 4. ***"Sometimes it is hard to know just where to draw the line with children. How much freedom do you allow your child?"***

Response	Respondents	Percentage (0 . . . 10 . . . 20 . . . 30 . . . 40 . . . 50 . . . 60 . . . 70)
Moderate or lots of freedom	346	31
Varies with the situation	307	28
Very strict or moderately strict	284	25
Average	176	16
Total	1,113	

of freedom. Nevertheless, they indicated that in a practical situation they did place restrictions on their children (see Fig. 24). When asked, for example, if there were children with whom they preferred that their own children not play, nearly two-thirds (63 per cent) of these same parents answered Yes.

FIGURE 24

Parental Restrictions on Playmates

Question 4-c. ***"Are there some children with whom you would prefer that your child not play?"***

Response	Respondents	Percentage (0 . . . 10 . . . 20 . . . 30 . . . 40 . . . 50 . . . 60 . . . 70)
Yes	692	63
No	415	37
Total	1,107	

FIGURE 25

Care of Children by Outsiders

Question 6-c. ***"Is there anyone outside the family who regularly has much to do with the care and upbringing of the children?"***

Response	Respondents	Percentage (0 . . . 10 . . . 20 . . . 30 . . . 40 . . . 50 . . . 60 . . . 70)
Child's grandparent(s)	248	62
Person not a relative	67	17
Relative other than grandparent	58	14
Agency	27	7
Total	400	

ARRANGEMENTS FOR CHILD CARE

The parents were asked if anyone outside the immediate family regularly took care of the children. The responses (see Fig. 25) showed that child care was mainly the job of the parents, 59 per cent reporting that no outsiders had a part in the upbringing of their children. When persons outside the immediate family were involved, they were usually the child's grandparents. These responses indicate that it was not lack of opportunity that prevented parents from turning to their own parents for help with their problems in child rearing. Although in this research sample there were 248 instances in which grandparents were actually

FIGURE 26

Characteristics of the Ideal Child

Question 7. ***"None of us are perfect, of course, and neither are our children. But what do you consider to be the ideal characteristics of a child of elementary-school age?"***

Response	Respondents	Percentage 0...10...20...30...40...50...60...70
Obedience, good behavior	311	29
Good interpersonal relations	175	16
Intelligence, educational achievement	162	15
Honesty, fairness, truthfulness	88	8
Compassion, consideration	87	8
Independent, self-reliant	66	6
Happy, contented	58	5
Physical health, appearance	51	5
Respect for parents, authority	50	5
Emotionally well-adjusted	35	3
Total	1,083	

involved with the care of the child, only 5 per cent of the subjects, as we have already noted, listed their own parents as a source of help for solving their problems.

Of the 400 parents who said that some outsider had a part in the care of their children, 70 per cent stated that this arrangement did not cause trouble. In view of clinical experience with situations in which an outsider has some responsibility for the care of the child, it seems unlikely that the incidence of problems would actually be so small in this group. Perhaps those parents who used outsiders to help care for their children felt some guilt about the arrangement and therefore could not bring themselves to admit that problems had arisen as a result.

IDEAL CHARACTERISTICS OF CHILDREN AND PARENTS

The last section of the interview, concerned with the subjects' concept of the characteristics of the ideal child and the ideal parent, evoked a wide variety of responses. For the ideal child (see Fig. 26) the charac-

FIGURE 27

Characteristics of the Ideal Parent

Question 7-d. ***"What do you think are the most important characteristics a person should have to be a good parent?"***

Response	Respondents	Percentage (0...10...20...30...40...50...60...70)
Patience and perseverance	327	31
Love of and interest in children	219	21
Understanding	205	20
Moral values	171	16
Tolerance	53	5
Well-adjusted	39	4
Other	33	3
Total	1,047	

teristic most frequently mentioned as desirable was obedience—seemingly a correlate of the fact that disobedience had been listed as the most frequent cause for punishment. The only other characteristics often mentioned were good interpersonal relations and intelligence. The parental responses to this question tend to support the observations of those who point out the increasing emphasis being placed on conformity and group orientation as desirable attributes in American culture, for good behavior and getting along well with others were stressed as ideal characteristics by these parents, while such individualistic concepts as honesty and self-reliance were seldom mentioned.

For the ideal parent (see Fig. 27) the most admired characteristic was patience, the very trait which many subjects had said (on an earlier question) that they personally lacked. Having a love of children and an understanding of children were also mentioned by a substantial number of respondents as being important characteristics.

SUMMARY

This group of subjects seemed to be very much aware of their own role as parents and quite concerned about their adequacy for it.[1] They felt that their actions and attitudes were important in their parent-child relations. When problems arose, these parents were inclined to try to solve them by attempting to change their own behavior rather than that of the child, in spite of the fact that most of the parents viewed the child's behavior as the immediate cause of trouble in most instances.

Obedience and discipline were consistently seen as problem areas by this group of parents. They were reluctant to punish their children, but when they did, their reasons were likely to be associated with problems of discipline. The most frequently used method of punishment was spanking.

Although some anxiety was connected with their role of parenthood, having problems did not make the subjects feel different or unusual, for they considered their problems to be common to most families. Although they worried about their own adequacy as parents, most of them felt that their methods of solving problems and their types of punishment were

[1] For remarkably similar results on a carefully selected nationwide sample, see G. Gurin, J. Veroff, and Sheila Feld, *Americans View Their Mental Health* (New York, Basic Books, 1960).

effective. Further evidence that this was a group of normal families is the fact that very few of them described specific symptoms in their children.

The majority of these parents enjoyed the love and companionship of their children, but not many of them felt highly effective in this area. Meeting the child's needs, particularly his physical needs, did not seem to be much of a problem for the parents, but neither was it a source of satisfaction to them to be able to do it. Ironically, the things these parents could do best they apparently did not enjoy, whereas the things they most enjoyed they did not seem to be very good at doing.

These parents turned to their contemporaries for help with their problems of child rearing, not to the older generation. Since the fact that they did not rely on their own parents for help was not due to lack of opportunity, it can be concluded that most parents feel the older generation's methods of child rearing are not the answer for today's changing culture. The influence of group orientation was also evident in the expression of what they considered the ideal child. These parents stressed conformity concepts—such as obedience and ability to get along well with others—and practically ignored the more individualistic ideals, such as self-reliance and honesty.

IX

Determinants of Parental Attitudes

BEFORE WE COULD TEST THE HYPOTHESES OF THIS STUDY, we had to find the answers to two important questions.

First, were the subjects in the four research categories approximately equal on the various measures before the intervening educational method was introduced? If differences did exist among the groups, these differences would have to be taken into account in the analysis of any changes that occurred. Although the subjects for all categories (except those in the Lecture-Control Group) were obtained from the same school districts at the same time in an effort to make the groups comparable, the subjects in the different groups were not individually matched. Neither could the groups, with the possible exception of the Random-Control Group, be considered true random samples in the statistical sense. Thus, the fact that the research categories were considered as intact groups with differential treatment made it imperative to compare the groups on the initial measurements.

Second, were there some important uncontrolled variables that exerted an influence on parental attitudes and behavior? To evaluate properly the intervening variable (in this case, the discussion method), it was necessary to know what other variables were also operating on attitudes and behavior. Variables such as age, sex, and socioeconomic status seemed likely to have some bearing on attitudes and behavior. The influence of such factors had to be taken into account in the analysis of changes that occurred.

COMPARISON OF RESEARCH GROUPS

A comparison of the scores on the initial Parent-Attitude Survey for subjects on which data were complete in the various research groups is presented in Table 9. The original group used to standardize this instrument is included for comparison, although this group was not a part of the research design. All groups scored above the midpoint of the scales, which was zero for each scale, since the possible range of scores was from −30 to +30. Similarly, all groups scored substantially higher on Causation and Understanding than on the other three scales. These results are a function of the scales themselves; that is, there is no reason to assume that the midpoint of the possible range of scores would be the true middle of the dimension being measured. Thus, a score of 14 or 15 on Causation or Understanding would have about the same significance as a score of 6 or 7 on one of the other three scales.

The group used for standardizing the instrument was not radically different from the four research groups, although the parents in it did score slightly lower on the first two scales than did those in the research groups. One way in which the composition of groups differed was that most of the standardization-group parents were from a small town, while the research-group parents were all city-dwellers.

Within the research groups, the only one that was consistently different from the others was the Lecture-Control Group. This group scored higher than the others on all but the first scale, and on Acceptance appeared to be substantially higher. The Lecture-Control Group differed from the others in that the lecture series were all held in large schools

TABLE 9

Group Means for Initial Parent-Attitude Survey

		Group Means Parent-Attitude Survey Scales				
Research Groups	No. of Subjects	Confidence	Causation	Acceptance	Understanding	Trust
Experimental	363	5.19	13.17	6.89	15.49	7.56
Lecture-Control	91	5.96	15.59	8.41	16.81	8.95
Nonattendant-Control	138	6.80	14.08	7.50	15.49	7.47
Random-Control	256	6.17	13.68	6.96	14.73	7.17
Standardization[1]	72	4.56	12.40	6.42	14.44	7.44

[1] This group was not a part of the research design.

serving a middle-class social level, whereas the other groups were drawn from schools that covered the entire socioeconomic range.

To determine whether the differences that existed among the research groups on the initial Parent-Attitude Survey were statistically significant, an analysis of variance was computed on these data. This method permits the simultaneous comparison of several groups to determine whether existing differences are greater than could be expected from random sampling or measurement errors. To refine the test further,[1] the four major research groups were subdivided into the following ten categories. The Experimental Group and the Lecture-Control Group were each divided into three categories: parents who attended one or two discussion meetings, those who attended three or four, and those who attended five or six. The Nonattendant-Control Group was divided into two categories: those parents who had registered for the discussion program, and those who had registered for the lecture program. The Random-Control Group was also divided into two categories: parents selected from schools where the discussion program was held, and those from schools where the lecture series took place.

Four of the five scales showed no differences among the research categories, but a statistically significant (.05 level)[2] difference appeared on the Acceptance scale. A study of the group means showed that this difference was due to the fact that the groups from the schools in which the lecture series took place had higher means on this scale than the other groups. This observation held true for all the groups from the lecture-series schools, regardless of their research category. Therefore it was determined that the research groups were not strictly comparable, at least on one of the attitude scales, before the intervening variable was introduced.

The same question regarding equivalence of the research groups applied to the initial data for children as well as to those for parents. The results of the initial measurements with children, from both the sociometric

[1] The results of this analysis of variance are presented in full in Appendix B, Table B-1.

[2] The level of statistical significance is a measure of the confidence placed in the results obtained. The .05 level of confidence indicates that such results could have occurred by chance alone only 1 time in 20. The .01 level means that similar results could have occurred by chance 1 time in 100, and the .001 level means 1 time in 1,000. The .05 level is the lowest usually accepted as indicating statistically significant results.

TABLE 10

Group Means for Initial Sociometric Evaluation and Teacher Rating

Research Groups	No. of Subjects	Group Means: Sociometric Evaluation	Group Means: Teacher Rating
Experimental	393	0.01	4.74
Lecture-Control	101	0.02	5.00
Nonattendant-Control	185	0.01	4.93
Random-Control	309	—0.02	4.75

[3] See Appendix B. The results of the analysis of variance for the sociometric data are presented in Table B-4, and those for the teacher rating in Table B-5. These two analyses of variance also included the variables (other than research category) of socioeconomic level and sex, discussed in this chapter.

evaluation and the teacher rating, are presented in Table 10. The mean sociometric scores for all the various research groups were very close to zero, which was automatically the mean for this measurement since the scores were standard scores. These scores could vary in either a positive or negative direction; and one group, the Random-Control, was slightly below the mean.

The true mean for the teacher rating was 5.0, since these numbers represent ranks, with a possible range from 1 to 9 and a forced normalized distribution. Note that on the teacher rating the lower the numerical score (or rank), the better a child's adjustment to the classroom situation, since a rank of 1 stood for the best adjustment and that of 9 for the poorest. The mean ranks for all the different research groups were quite close to the true mean, despite some variation.

While these differences in the children's data were small, they were checked nevertheless for statistical significance by the same analysis of variance used to analyze initial differences in the measurements with parents.[3] The results showed no significant differences among the children in the various research groups at the beginning of the study.

VARIABLES OF AGE, SEX, AND SOCIOECONOMIC STATUS

Since the hypotheses of the research design concerned the influence of the discussion method (the experimental variable) on parent attitudes, it was important to know what other variables were related to these attitudes. Variables such as age, sex, and socioeconomic status are usually considered as important determinants of the attitudes of parents. To investigate the importance of these variables in the present research sample, two more analyses of variance were computed on the initial data from the Parent-Attitude Survey. This time the entire research sample was divided into other categories irrespective of their classification in the research category.

The first of these studies concerned the relation of the age of the child to parental attitudes. Age was divided into seven intervals by years: 6 and under, 7, 8, 9, 10, 11, and 12 and above.[4]

The age of the child proved to be significantly (.001 level) related to parent attitudes as measured by three of the scales—Acceptance, Trust, and Causation. The group means for each age-level, on which this analysis of variance was based, showed a consistent relation on all three of the scales—the younger the child, the higher the parent's score on the scale. Parents of younger children showed more acceptance of them, trusted them more, and were more inclined to regard environment as the cause of their behavior than did the parents of older children. Thus, the age of the child, which was not controlled in the selection of the groups (other than the limitation that all children were of elementary-school age) was an important factor in determining some parent attitudes.

The second of these studies was a three-way analysis of variance.[5] This technique permitted the study of three independent variables at the same time, and also yielded information on the interaction of the variables with each other. Here the three variables were the socioeconomic level (using the school district as a rough index), the sex of the child, and the sex of the parent. The school districts[6] in which the parents lived were grouped into three socioeconomic categories—high, middle, and low—on the basis of observation and knowledge of the community. The sex variables (for parent and for child) each had two categories, of course.

The extremely strong influence that socioeconomic status exerts on parental attitudes was clearly demonstrated by this analysis, even though the index used (school district) was very gross. This variable

[4] See Appendix B, Table B-2 for the results of this analysis.

[5] *Ibid.*, Table B-3.

[6] The Negro schools were not used in this analysis because too few Negro fathers were included in the sample.

reached a high level of statistical significance (.001) on every scale of the Parent-Attitude Survey. Without exception, the group means showed that the relation between socioeconomic status and attitude scores was positive, i.e., the higher the parent's socioeconomic status, the higher his attitude scores.

The sex of the parent also proved to be significantly related to attitudes on all the scales except Confidence. Acceptance and Trust showed the strongest relation (.001 level), but Causation and Understanding were also statistically significant at a lower level. The relation of this variable to parent attitudes, as shown by the group means, was the same on all four scales; and mothers had higher scores than fathers.

The third variable in this analysis—the sex of the child—seemed to have no relation to parent attitudes. None of the differences in the group means were significant on any of the scales.

Of the fifteen two-way interactions only two were significant. Each was a socioeconomic-level and sex-of-parent interaction, one on the Causation scale and the other on the Understanding scale. This interaction means that the relation between parent attitudes (on these two scales) and socioeconomic level is different for fathers and mothers. The group means showed that the fathers' attitudes were more strongly influenced by their socioeconomic status than were the mothers' attitudes. None of the three-way interactions was significant.

These two analyses of variance, using the entire research sample with the five scales from the initial Parent-Attitude Survey as the dependent variables, clearly showed the existence of some significant uncontrolled independent variables related to parental attitudes, in which socioeconomic status was of particular importance.

We also investigated the possibility that there were uncontrolled variables which were related to the initial data collected from children. Two variables were studied, socioeconomic level (using the school districts, grouped in the same manner as for the parent data, plus a fourth category of Negro schools) and sex of the child. Age was not included since this variable was controlled by the nature of the measurements. That is, both the teacher rating and the sociometric device were intraclass measures, and all the children within a given class were approximately the same age.

The results of these two analyses of variance showed only the sex of the child to be related to the sociometric scores and the teacher ratings (.05 level for sociometric scores; .01 level for the teacher ratings). In both instances girls had higher scores than boys, results which were consistent with those of preliminary studies made during the development of these two measuring devices. Thus, the sex of the subject proved to be an important uncontrolled variable in the children's data, although it was not a significant factor in the data from parents.

FACTOR ANALYSIS OF THE INITIAL DATA

The analysis of variance studies on the initial data collected from parents and children showed the existence of variables which were strongly related to the areas under study but which had not been precisely controlled in the research design. To obtain a more accurate appraisal of the uncontrolled variables and to insure that no others had been overlooked, a factor analysis was made on 613 families in which data were complete for every type of measurement and information used in this Project. Factor analysis is a procedure whereby the major underlying dimensions of measurement can be "pulled out" of a related group of scores on the same subjects. Every score, or variable, is correlated[7] with every other score.

Where a number of these variables form a cluster of high intercorrelations there is evidence that a factor, or dimension of measurement common to these variables, exists in the data. This method also permits the determination of the factor loading (the extent to which a variable is related to the factor) for each variable on each factor. Thus, it is possible to select the variable with the highest factor loading to serve as a "marker" variable, or rough index of that factor in future studies.

All the quantitative data collected on parents and children were used in the factor analysis, a total of 36 variables.[8] In addition to the scores from the various measurement devices, these variables included identification material and home and neighborhood ratings made at the time of the interview. The ratings included such items as type of neighborhood, traffic density, spacing of dwelling units, play space for children, and the

[7] Product-moment correlations were used. These reduce to point-biserial correlation coefficients when one variable is dichotomous, as in the case of the sex variable.

[8] See Appendix B. The 36 variables used in the factor analysis are presented in Table B-6, and the intercorrelation matrix for the variables is presented in Table B-7.

condition of the neighborhood. The home was rated as to type (house, apartment, duplex), living space, condition, and comparison with other homes in the neighborhood. The identification material included the number of children in the family, the ages of the father and mother, their education, occupation, and religious affiliation and frequency of church attendance. Other information used in the factor analysis was the age, sex, and class grade of the child, school district, and the research category in which we had placed the family. The direction of some of the variables was reversed to give high scores a positive meaning; for example, the teacher-rating scores, in which a low numerical rank meant good adjustment, were reversed so that a high numerical score indicated good adjustment.

The centroid method of factoring was used on the intercorrelations of these 36 variables. The first 11 factors[9] to emerge accounted for all but 3 per cent of the estimated common variance among the variables, and the computations were terminated at this point. Of these 11, Factors I, III, V, and XI were measurement factors defined entirely by combinations of scores from the various measurement devices. Since these were to be the dependent variables in future studies, there was no necessity to control or allow for these 4 factors and they were not considered further. The other 7 factors follow: Housing (Factor II), Age of Child (Factor IV), Age of Parents (Factor VI), Neighborhood (Factor VII), Research Category (Factor VIII), Sex of Child (Factor IX), and Socioeconomic Level (Factor X).

These 7 factors were reduced to 4 by hand rotation of the reference axes, and the most representative variable for each of these 4 factors was selected[10] as a marker variable to be controlled in subsequent analyses. In this manner, the variable of the father's education (No. 27) was chosen to represent the major variation in socioeconomic level. The age of the child (No. 4) and the sex of the child (No. 3) served as marker variables for factors defined primarily by age and sex. The factor of research cate-

[9] See Appendix B, Table B-8, for the factor loadings on each of the 11 factors.

[10] The rotations were designed to maximize the number of near-zero loadings, which helped to identify the most representative marker variables. The markers were selected not only for their high loading on their own factor, but also for low loadings on the other factors. This choice was essentially an arbitrary one, and in some instances other variables might serve equally well. Also, a single variable cannot represent completely an entire factor. In this instance, however, it was possible to find marker variables with a high loading on one factor and relatively low loadings on the others.

gory was, of course, represented by the research-category variable (No. 2). These 4 variables (father's education, age of the child, sex of the child, and research category) were used as the independent variables in the tests of the research hypotheses described in the next chapter.

The factor analysis completed the study of the initial measurements, and, along with the analyses of variance, provided the information needed for a valid test of the hypotheses of the research design. These preliminary studies determined that the various research groups were not precisely equivalent before the intervening variable being evaluated (the discussion-group method) was introduced, although the differences appeared to be small. Also, these studies isolated three important uncontrolled variables that were related to the attitudes and behavior being measured: socioeconomic level, age, and sex. While other uncontrolled variables may possibly have existed (factor analysis is by nature limited to the data on which it is performed), these three seemed to be the most important.

X

Results

All the preliminary efforts of the project were directed toward the major research purpose: to evaluate rigorously the effectiveness of group discussion as a method of changing parental attitudes and behavior. As outlined in Chapter V, the research design included two explicit hypotheses concerning the direct effects of the discussion method on parents and its indirect effects on their children. The studies described in the preceding chapters provided the information necessary to make valid statistical tests of these predictions.

Two classes of persons served as subjects in the research design: the parents, with whom the discussion method was used directly; and the children of these parents, who were assigned to the various research groups solely on the basis of their parents' placement therein. There was no program of any kind for children. Any changes that occurred in the children had to be the indirect result of changes that occurred in their parents.

The primary hypothesis concerned both parents and children. It was predicted that the parents' attendance at a series of group-discussion meetings would result in significant changes in their parental attitudes and behavior. These changes would be toward greater confidence in the parental role, more insight into the causation of the child's behavior, greater acceptance of their child's behavior and feelings, more effective communication between parent and child, and a stronger feeling of mutual trust. It was further predicted that these positive changes in parents would, in turn, result in better social adjustment for the children, as measured by the sociometric method and teachers' ratings of classroom adjustment.

Three control groups were included in the design to eliminate the possibility that observed changes in the parents and children of the Experimental Group could be due to anything other than the discussion method: (1) a Lecture-Control Group comprised of parents (and their children) who listened to a series of talks by experts on parent-child relations; (2) a Nonattendant-Control Group comprised of all parents (and their children) who signed up for the discussion-group program or for the lecture program but failed to participate; and (3) a Random-Control Group of parents drawn at random from the remaining families in the participating schools. In all four groups, the quantity of observed change in attitudes and behavior was defined as the difference between the initial and the final measurements on the various instruments employed.

The secondary hypothesis was concerned with only the parents in the Experimental Group. It was predicted that the number of meetings attended, the degree of participation in the discussion, and the frequency with which personal references were made would all be directly related to the quantity of change shown by these parents.

FINDINGS CONCERNING PARENTS

PARENTAL ATTITUDES

Analysis of covariance was employed to test the hypothesis that attitudes of the parents in the Experimental Group changed significantly more than did those of the three control groups. This method corrects for any differences that existed among the groups initially, thereby insuring that the outcome is a direct result of the major intervening variable (the discussion method, lecture method, or nothing) rather than of initial differences between groups. The Experimental Group was divided into two parts according to the number of dicussion meetings attended, making five groups altogether for research categories. Part I was comprised of parents who attended one or two meetings, and Part II of parents who attended three or more.

In addition to these five groups constituting the research categories in the design, three other independent variables were taken into account systematically—age of child, sex of child, and socioeconomic level as indicated roughly by the father's education. These three variables had been selected as marker variables for the major factors discovered from the correlation and factor analysis described in Chapter IX. Their inclusion in the analysis of covariance insured adequate coverage of other variables that determine parental attitudes and behavior. Age of child had two intervals: 9 years or below, and above 9 years. Socioeconomic level was based on father's education divided into three intervals: no

TABLE 11

Analysis of Covariance for Research Category, Socioeconomic Level, Child's Age, and Child's Sex, Using the Five Attitude Scales as Dependent Variables
(648 Subjects)

Source of Variation	Degrees of Freedom	Confidence F[1]	*p*	Causation F[1]	*p*	Acceptance F[1]	*p*	Understanding F[1]	*p*	Trust F[1]	*p*
		Scales from Parent-Attitude Survey									
A Research Category	4	2.14	. .	3.09	.05	5.21	.001	3.34	.01	3.42	.01
B Socioeconomic Level	2	12.29	.001	7.46	.001	6.52	.01	13.23	.001	6.52	.01
C Child's Age	1			3.53	. .	2.48	. .	1.29	. .		
D Child's Sex	1			4.54	.05					4.93	.05
AB Interaction	8	2.04	.05	1.71	. .	1.72	. .	1.42	. .		
AC Interaction	4	3.42	.01	6.55	.001	2.67	.05	1.44	. .		
AD Interaction	4	1.78	. .					1.54	. .		
BC Interaction	2	2.11	. .			2.44	. .	1.23	. .	2.89	. .
BD Interaction	2	1.67	. .	4.96	.01	1.90	. .	2.30	. .	3.04	.05
CD Interaction	1										
ABC Interaction	8					1.02	. .			1.17	. .
ABD Interaction	8	1.12	. .	1.46	. .	1.36	. .	1.45	. .	1.02	. .
BCD Interaction	2					1.53	. .			1.01	. .
ACD Interaction	4	2.19									
ABCD Interaction	8										

[1] F-ratios less than 1.0 have been omitted.

education beyond high school, some college training, and graduation from college.

The resulting four-way design for analysis of covariance had a total of 60 categories or cells, one for each possible combination of the 4 independent factors. Separate analyses were carried out for each of the five scales in the Parent-Attitude Survey. All possible sources of variation were tested for significance, using the adjusted within-cell error variance in the denominator of the F-ratio and the appropriate mean-square estimate of each source of variation in the numerator. The results of these analyses of covariance are summarized in Table 11.

The research category—the variable of primary interest—proved significant for all but one of the attitude scales. The level of significance ranged from .05 for Causation to .001 for Acceptance. The mean changes that occurred for each of the groups as a result of the intervening variable (discussion, lecture, nothing) are illustrated in Figures 28–32. Parts I and II of the Experimental Group showed very similar quantities of change from initial to final scores, indicating that the frequency of attendance at the discussion groups did not matter so long as the parent attended at least once or twice. Consequently, the means in the figures are based on the Experimental Group as a whole.

The graphs reveal that the Experimental Group changed significantly more than any of the three control groups. On Acceptance (Fig. 30), for example, parents attending the discussion groups showed a mean change from 6.8 to 9.4, a gain of almost three points. By contrast, parents attending a lecture series or nothing at all either showed no mean change or a slight drop in score rather than an increase. Clearly, the principal hypothesis concerning the effect of the discussion method on parental attitudes has been confirmed.

FIGURE 28

Initial and Final Means for Confidence

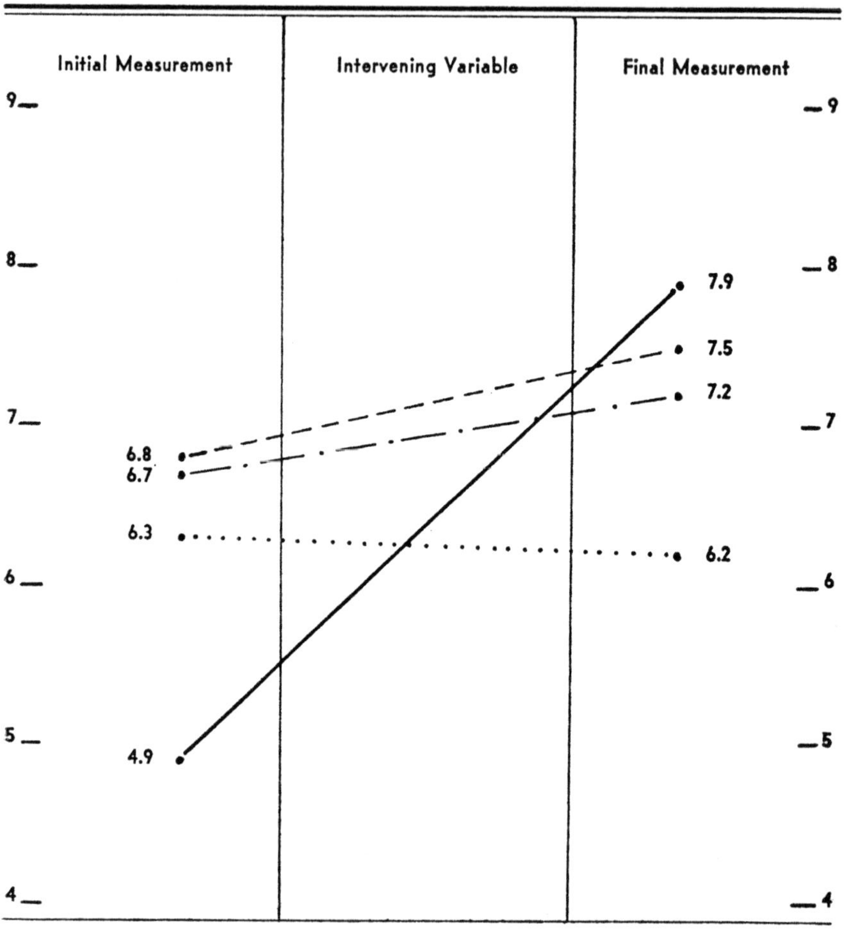

Legend

	Group	Intervening Variable
———————	Experimental	Discussion series
• • • • • • • • • •	Lecture Control	Lecture series
— — — — — —	Nonattendance Control	Nothing
—— • —— • ——	Random Control	Nothing

FIGURE 29

Initial and Final Means for *Causation*

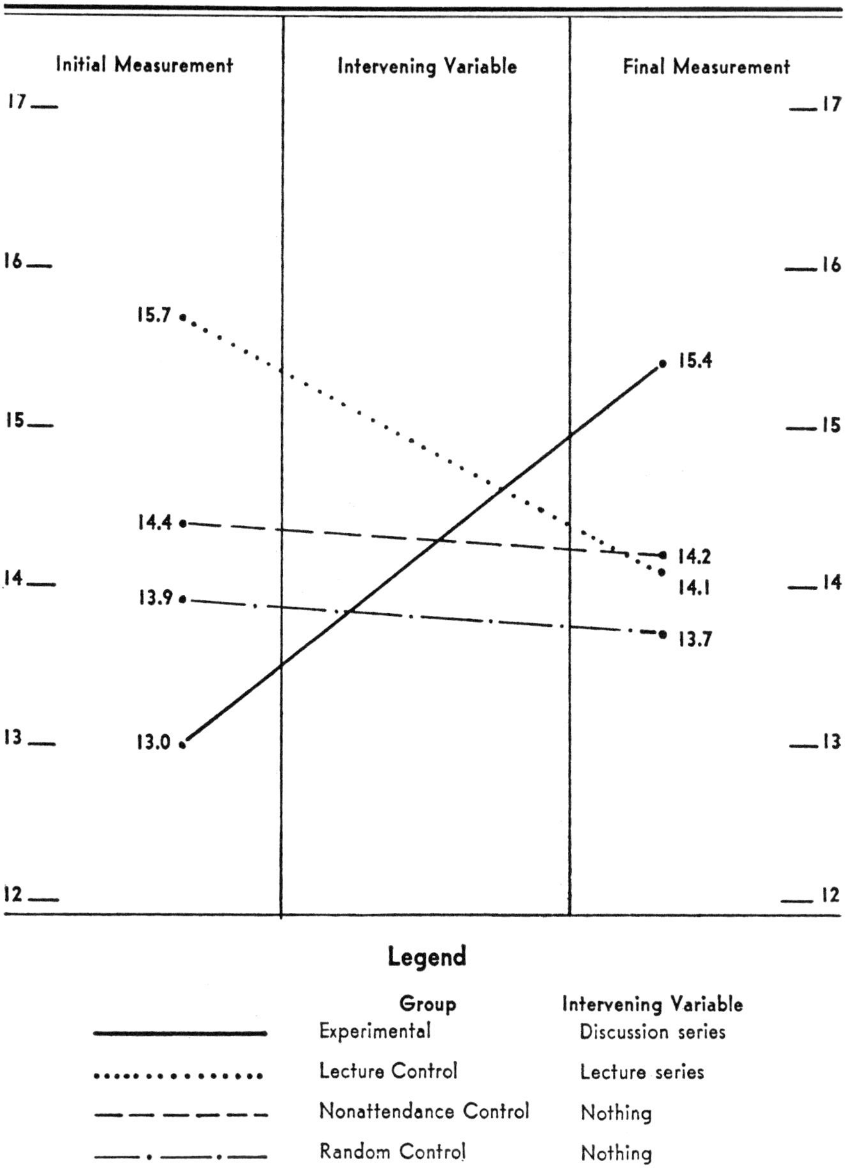

FIGURE 30

Initial and Final Means for *Acceptance*

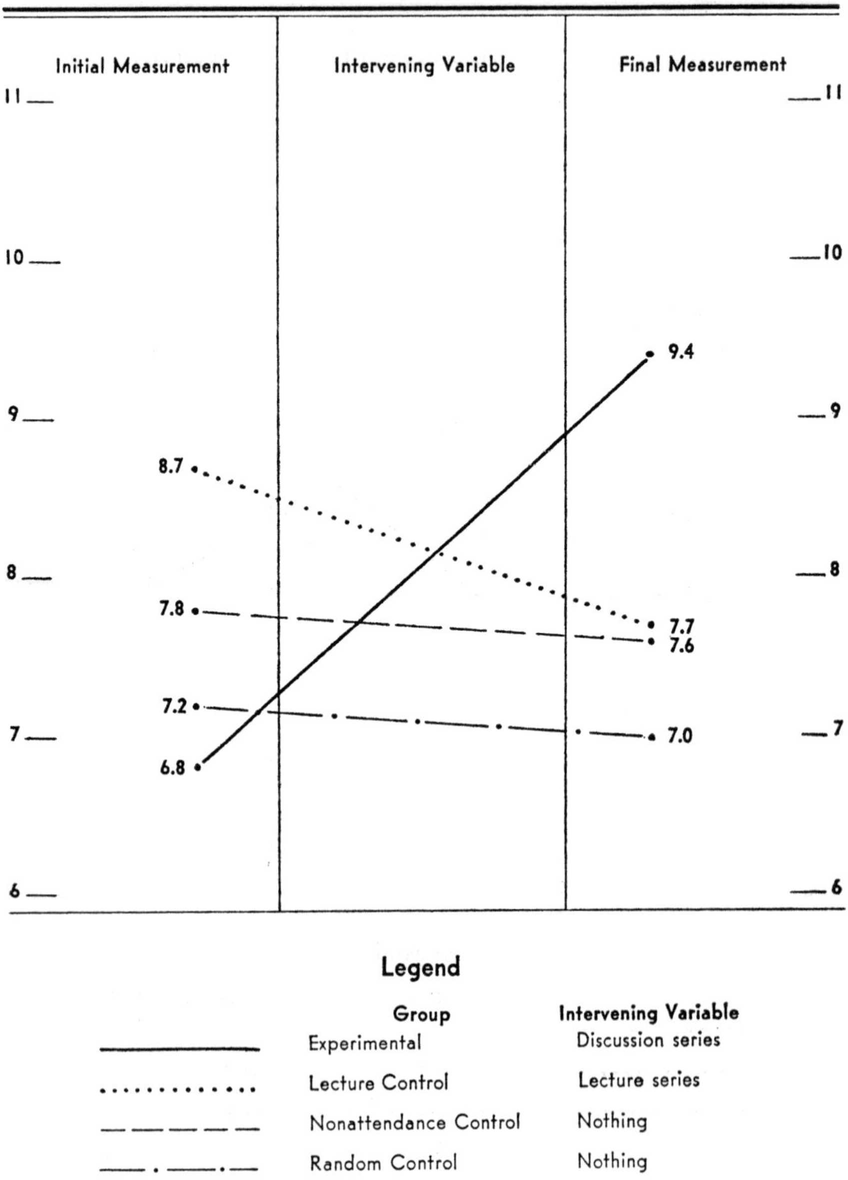

FIGURE 31

Initial and Final Means for *Understanding*

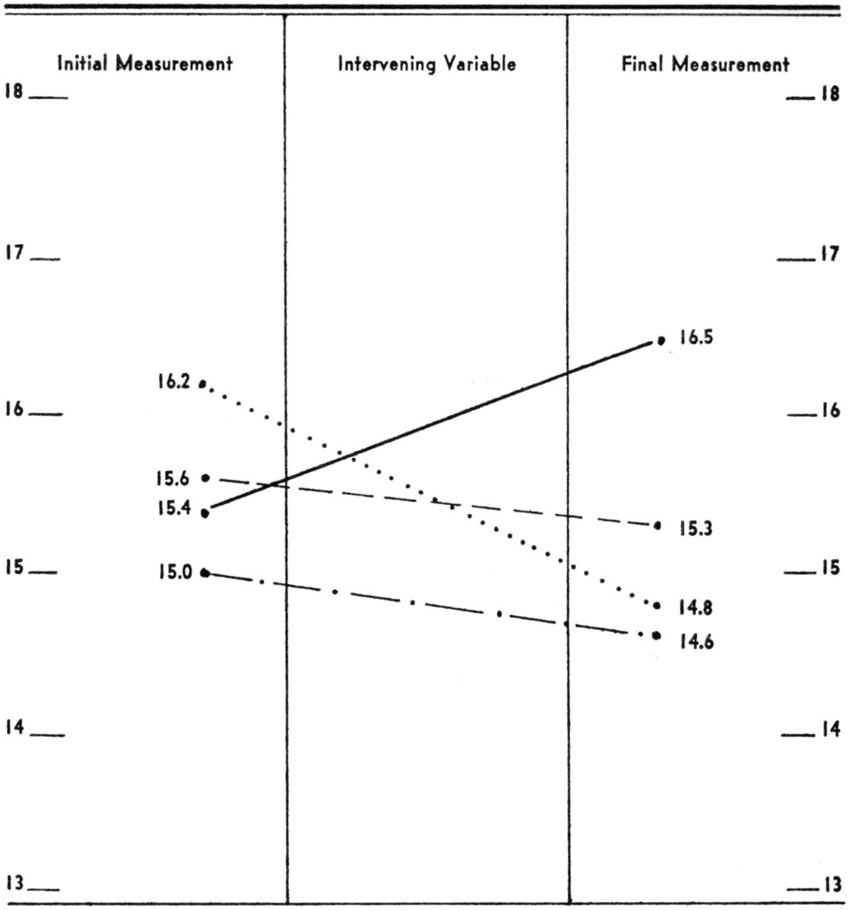

Legend

	Group	Intervening Variable
———————	Experimental	Discussion series
. . . .	Lecture Control	Lecture series
— — — — —	Nonattendance Control	Nothing
—— . —— . ——	Random Control	Nothing

FIGURE 32

Initial and Final Means for *Trust*

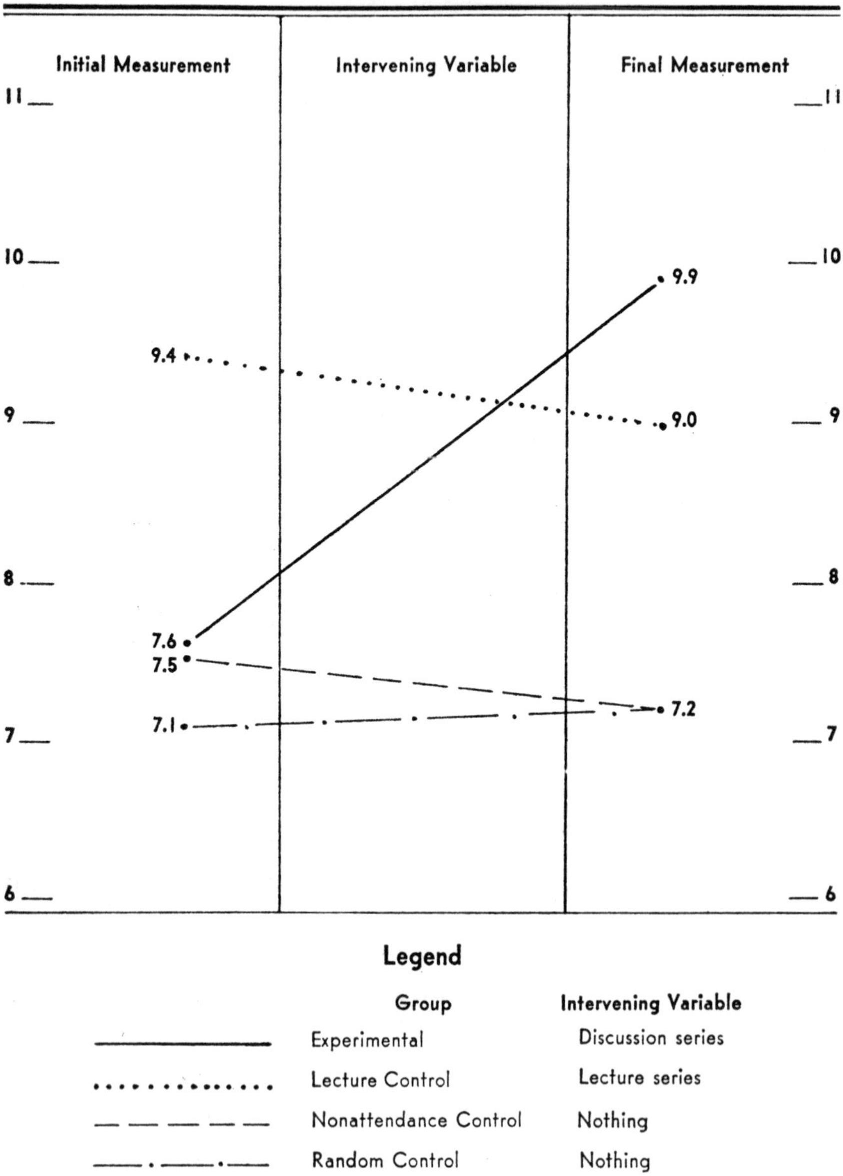

Socioeconomic level also proved to be strongly related to change in parental attitudes. All the scales showed a significant relation, at statistical levels ranging from .01 to .001. The group means for this variable showed that the lower socioeconomic group made the greatest gains. They were consistently higher on the final measurement than on the initial measurement on all five of the scales. The middle group remained about the same, and the upper socioeconomic group was slightly but consistently lower. Thus, no matter what research group they were in, parents from the lower socioeconomic level were more likely to improve their attitude scores than were parents from the other levels.[1]

The variable of age showed no significant results for any of the scales. The age of the child (within the limits of the elementary-school age range) was not related to change in his parent's attitudes, though this factor was related to the determination of these attitudes.

The sex of the child made a difference on two of the five scales—Causation and Trust—both at the .05 level. In both instances, the parents of boys had higher final scores than initial scores, while the scores of the parents of girls remained about the same. Parents of boys were more flexible in their attitudes in these two areas, changing more to the position that their son's behavior was the result of environment and also feeling that he could be trusted more.

Of the possible interactions between two variables, the combination of research category and socioeconomic level was significant on Confidence. The group means showed the influence of socioeconomic level to be much stronger on the Nonattendant and Random-Control Groups than on the Experimental or Lecture-Control Groups. In the two groups that were not exposed to any program, the lower socioeconomic levels improved their Confidence scores more than the upper level. In the groups that attended programs (discussion or lecture) the socioeconomic level had little effect on the quantity that occurred.

The interaction of research category and age seemed to exert the most influence on change of parental attitudes, reaching significance on three scales: Confidence, Causation, and Acceptance. On all three scales the

[1] In interpreting these results it should be kept in mind that the socioeconomic level strongly influenced the results of the initial measurement (see Chapter IX), with the upper socioeconomic levels having the highest scores. Thus, there may have been a measurement artifact involved; that is, the lower group had more room to move up on the scales than did the upper group.

pattern of group means was very similar. The variable of age exerted considerable influence in the control groups, usually the parents of younger children showing small negative changes and the parents of older children remaining about the same. By contrast, the Experimental Group showed positive changes on all three scales at both age levels, with little difference between the two. Thus, the influence of age was less important in the Experimental Group, where there were positive changes at both age levels, than it was in the control groups, where the direction of changes varied with the age of the child.

The only other significant two-way interaction was between socioeconomic level and sex on two of the scales: Causation and Trust. The attitudinal changes of the parents of boys were not related consistently to their socioeconomic status, but parents of girls did show this relation. All the means for parents of girls showed negative changes on these two scales, with the parents in the upper socioeconomic level showing greater negative changes than those in the lower socioeconomic level. The influence of the sex of the child on attitude change in these two areas was therefore shown to be related to the families' socioeconomic level. Parents of girls were more likely to be influenced by social-class factors in their attitudes regarding Causation and Trust than were parents of boys.

None of the three-way or four-way interactions was significant.

This analysis of covariance demonstrated quite clearly the effectiveness of the discussion method in changing parental attitudes. It also showed that some of the other variables studied, particularly the socioeconomic level, were related to change of attitudes, just as they were related to the formation of attitudes. However, these uncontrolled variables had less influence within the Experimental Group than with the other research categories, showing not only that the discussion method is effective, but that it is effective at all socioeconomic levels and is not influenced by the variables of age and sex.

PARENT-INTERVIEW RESPONSES

Just as with the Parent-Attitude Survey, the parent interview was also used to test the principal hypothesis of the study. Did the parents in the Experimental Group show more change than those in the control groups when they were interviewed the second time? By the use of the chi-square technique for testing the significance of differences of frequency

FIGURE 33

Initial and Final Responses of the Experimental Group to:

Question 1-c. ***"What do you think caused this situation* [described in Question 1] *to develop?"***

Response	Respondents	Initial Interview Percentage 0...20...40...60...	Respondents	Final Interview Percentage 0...20...40...60...
Parent's behavior or attitude	74	26	119	42
Inherent characteristic of children	47	17	39	14
Environmental situation	46	16	38	13
Age relation	46	16	36	13
Uncodable	30	10	23	8
Normal development, "stages"	16	6	21	7
Physical condition or health	9	3	7	3
Inherited traits	8	3	1	0
Culture, society	8	3	0	0
Total	284		284	

data it was possible to discover whether the various research groups differed significantly in the amount of change of response from the initial to the final interview.[2] The chi-square analysis of change of response of the Experimental Group and the three control groups for each interview question is summarized in Appendix B, Table B-9.

[2] The interview data were treated on a "changed response" or "unchanged response" basis from initial measurement to final measurement for each individual, which provided two columns for chi-square analysis. The rows were the four research categories. The expected frequencies for each cell of this 2 $\times$ 4 table were the products of the row and column totals divided by the total number of subjects. The observed frequencies were those actually noted (changed or unchanged) for each subject. The statistical test was whether or not the observed frequencies were significantly different from the expected frequencies.

FIGURE 34

Initial and Final Responses of the Experimental Group to:

Question 6-c. ***"Is there anyone outside the family who regularly has much to do with the care and upbringing of the children?"***

Response	Respondents	Initial Interview Percentage 0...20...40...60...	Respondents	Final Interview Percentage 0...20...40...60...
No	165	58	193	68
Child's grandparent(s)	63	22	53	19
Relative other than grandparent	22	8	16	6
Unrelated individual	19	7	13	4
Uncodable	9	3	7	2
Agency	4	1	2	1
Yes (unspecified)	2	1	0	0
Total	284		284	

The differences among the groups resulted in a significant chi square (beyond the .05 level) in 11 of the 23 questions tested. With only one exception the significant difference was due to greater change in the Experimental Group than in the control groups, again confirming the principal hypothesis of the research design.

Of perhaps even greater interest than the statistical proof that the discussion-group parents did change more than those in the control groups was the disposition of the changes that occurred. What were the differences in response given by parents who had attended the discussion meetings? The distributions of responses for the Experimental Group in the initial and final interviews are illustrated graphically in Figures 33–41, showing how these parents changed on the questions upon which they differed significantly from parents in the control groups.

One effect that the discussion groups had on parents was to increase the importance that parents attached to their own part in their parent-child relations. In the final interview many more of these parents blamed

FIGURE 35

Initial and Final Responses of the Experimental Group to:

Question 2. ***"A parent is expected to do many things—and make many decisions—as a part of the job of raising children. Some of these things are fun, some are not so much fun. As you think about it, what are the things that please you most about being a parent?"***

Response	Respondents	Initial Interview Percentage 0...20...40...60...	Respondents	Final Interview Percentage 0...20...40...60...
Companionship, love and affection	85	30	84	30
Interesting, meaningful experience	66	23	57	20
Achievement by the child	63	22	89	31
Meeting the child's needs	30	11	30	11
Uncodable	23	8	21	7
Help or contribution by child	17	6	3	1
Total	284		284	

themselves for their problems of child rearing than was the case for the control groups (Fig. 33). This increased importance given the parental role was also reflected in the fact that the number of parents who allowed outsiders to take care of their children had decreased (Fig. 34). After attending the discussion groups a substantial number of parents (twenty-eight) apparently canceled their child-care arrangements and took over the job themselves. Of those who continued to use outsiders to care for their children, fewer were satisfied with this arrangement after attending the discussion meetings (Question 6-*d*, not shown graphically). When interviewed initially, 73 per cent of the parents said their child-care arrangements caused no problems; after the discussion series only 61 per cent gave this response.

Attending the discussion groups also changed some of the parents' views about which phases of parenthood they most enjoyed. In the second

FIGURE 36

Initial and Final Responses of the Experimental Group to:

Question 1-a. ***"What have you done to help this situation [described in Question 1]?"***

Response	Respondents	Initial Interview Percentage 0...20...40...60...	Respondents	Final Interview Percentage 0...20...40...60...
Changed own behavior or attitude	70	25	109	38
Explanations, reasoning	63	22	55	19
Manipulated environment	42	15	25	9
Done nothing	29	10	11	4
Punishment	26	9	31	11
Sought outside help	26	9	27	9
Uncodable	25	9	19	7
Rewards or inducements	3	1	7	3
Total	284		284	

FIGURE 37

Initial and Final Responses of the Experimental Group to:

Question 5. ***"Sometimes it is necessary to punish a child. What method of punishment do you usually use?"***

Response	Respondents	Initial Interview Percentage 0...20...40...60...	Respondents	Final Interview Percentage 0...20...40...60...
Corporal punishment	146	51	105	37
Withdrawal of privileges	59	21	84	30
Confinement	41	15	59	21
Verbal	35	12	33	11
Uncodable	2	1	2	1
Does not punish	1	o	1	o
Total	284		284	

FIGURE 38

Initial and Final Responses of the Experimental Group to:

Question 1-*b*. ***"How has this [action described in Question 1-a] worked out?"***

Response	Respondents	Initial Interview Percentage (0 . . . 20 . . . 40 . . . 60 . . .)	Respondents	Final Interview Percentage (0 . . . 20 . . . 40 . . . 60 . . .)
Great improvement	24	8	28	10
Improvement	101	36	112	40
Slight improvement	86	30	95	33
No change	39	14	22	8
Made matters worse	3	1	1	0
Uncodable	31	11	26	9
Total	284		284	

FIGURE 39

Initial and Final Responses of the Experimental Group to:

Question 5-*c*. ***"How do these methods [of punishment] work?"***

Response	Respondents	Initial Interview Percentage (0 . . . 20 . . . 40 . . . 60 . . .)	Respondents	Final Interview Percentage (0 . . . 20 . . . 40 . . . 60 . . .)
Effective or very effective	139	49	151	53
Effective (qualified)	108	38	113	40
Not effective	32	11	14	5
Uncodable	5	2	6	2
Total	284		284	

FIGURE 40

Initial and Final Responses of the Experimental Group to:

Question 1-e. ***"Have you ever sought outside help in this matter [described in Question 1]?"***

Response	Respondents	Initial Interview Percentage 0...20...40...60...	Respondents	Final Interview Percentage 0...20...40...60...
No outside help	111	39	156	55
Friend or neighbor	47	17	36	13
Teacher or school personnel	44	15	29	10
Physician	37	13	29	10
Uncodable	19	7	21	8
Professional agency	14	5	9	3
Member of family, relative	8	3	3	1
Individual specialist or practitioner other than physician	4	1	1	0
Total	284		284	

interview more parents listed the child's achievements as the most gratifying result of parenthood, and fewer gave the response of "help from the child" (Fig. 35). There was no change in the desire for love and companionship, however; this was a popular response in both interviews.

Not only did parents' attitudes about parent-child relations shift as a result of attending the discussion groups, but their behavior toward their children changed also. When asked the second time what they did about their child-rearing problems (Fig. 36), more parents responded that they changed their own attitudes or behavior. This behavioral change was consistent with the attitudinal change noted earlier, where more parents felt their own attitudes and behavior were the cause of their child-rearing problems. Some discussion-group parents also changed their methods of punishment (Fig. 37); after the discussion series fewer parents used

FIGURE 41

Initial and Final Responses of the Experimental Group to:

Question 3. ***"What are the things that worry you most about being a parent?"***

Response	Respondents	Initial Interview Percentage 0...20...40...60...	Respondents	Final Interview Percentage 0...20...40...60...
Own adequacy	68	24	84	30
Physical: illness, accidents	51	18	30	11
How child will turn out, character development	50	18	61	21
Behavior and activity of child	24	8	10	4
Uncodable	23	8	15	5
Finances	18	6	24	8
Specific problems or symptoms	16	6	13	5
No worries	10	4	17	6
Education, school grades	9	3	12	4
Undesirable environmental situation	9	3	7	2
Separation, broken home	3	1	8	3
Religious or spiritual	3	1	3	1
Total	284		284	

corporal punishment and more used the withdrawal of privileges and, to a lesser extent, confinement as a means of punishment.

These changes in handling problems and methods of punishment apparently worked out satisfactorily for the discussion-group parents. In both areas parents gave more effective ratings to their methods after attending the discussion groups (Figs. 38, 39). Perhaps as a result of their greater satisfaction with the way they were handling their problems with their children, fewer parents sought outside help after they had at-

FIGURE 42

Initial and Final Responses of the Lecture-Control Group to:

Question 3. ***"What are the things that worry you most about being a parent?"***

Response	Respondents	Initial Interview Percentage 0...20...40...60...	Respondents	Final Interview Percentage 0...20...40...60...
Own adequacy	8	11	21	29
Physical: illness, accidents	12	17	14	19
How child will turn out, character development	24	33	17	24
Behavior and activity of child	1	1	0	0
Uncodable	7	10	8	11
Finances	5	7	3	4
Specific problems or symptoms	3	4	2	3
No worries	1	1	2	3
Education, school grades	4	6	1	1
Undesirable environmental situation	4	6	2	3
Separation, broken home	3	4	2	3
Religious	0	0	0	0
Total	72		72	

tended the discussion groups (Fig. 40). The discussion groups appeared to have provided all the help needed by many parents.

Despite the changes in attitudes and behavior, and the greater satisfaction with their methods of child rearing, the discussion groups increased the number of parents who were concerned about their own adequacy as a parent (Fig. 41). However, this change was even more marked in the parents who attended the series of lectures (Fig. 42) than in those attending the discussions. In both groups, the response "own adequacy" was given more frequently as a source of worry by parents after they had attended their respective educational programs. Perhaps increased concern about self-adequacy is a natural consequence—at least the desired goal—of any attempt to educate parents in parent-child relations. The significant difference in the two groups in this instance was that the discussion-group parents did something about their increased concern—they changed their behavior—whereas the lecture-series parents did not.

The chi-square analysis of the Parent Interview confirmed the results obtained by analysis of covariance of the Parent-Attitude Survey. Parents who attended the discussion meetings *did* indicate changes in their attitudes and behavior, and these changes were significantly greater than changes in the control groups. The fact that positive changes were demonstrable on two different kinds of measurements (attitude scales and interview material) is additional evidence of the effectiveness of the group-discussion method.

EFFECT OF ATTENDANCE, PARTICIPATION, AND PERSONAL REFERENCE

As indicated at the beginning of this chapter, the second set of hypotheses concerned only parents in the Experimental Group, and had to do with three variables: the number of discussion meetings attended; the amount of participation in the discussion; and the extent to which the parent made references about himself. In each case, it was predicted that the higher a parent rated on the variable, the greater would be the changes that occurred in his attitudes and behavior.

The test of the attendance variable is presented in Appendix B, Table B-10. Chi square was again used, substituting the number of meetings attended in place of research groups. Three categories were used: parents who attended one or two meetings; those who attended three or four; and those who attended five or six.

The number of meetings attended did not influence change of response to any great extent, since only 2 of the 23 questions reached statistical significance. A high attendance score strengthened the behavioral shift previously noted in the Experimental Group for Question 1-*a* ("Parental Response to Difficulties"). A greater percentage of parents who attended five or six meetings recorded changes in their own attitudes and behavior as a way of meeting problems. Similarly, those who attended many of the meetings more often indicated that they did not seek outside help with their problems (Question 1-*e*). For all the rest of the questions, however, the number of meetings attended made no difference.

The degree of participation in the discussion was measured by counting the actual number of comments a parent made during the course of the discussion meetings.[3] We then divided parents into four categories according to the amount of participation, and a chi-square test of the differences among these categories was computed for the degree of change in each pair of items across the two interviews (see Appendix B, Table B-11).

The frequency of participation in the discussion also had little influence in changing the parents' response. Only one question (Question 1-*c*) showed a significant difference among the categories. This difference was in the predicted direction, however: it was those parents who participated more freely in the discussions who responded more frequently in the second interview that it was their own attitudes and behavior that caused their difficulties in child rearing.

The last variable expected to have a positive effect on change of attitude and behavior—personal references—was measured by counting the number of statements a parent made which included one or more personal references. This number was divided by the total number of comments made by the individual, yielding a score based on the percentage of personal references. These scores were used to separate the Experimental Group into four categories, ranging from a high degree of personal reference to a low, and the chi-square test was again applied to the resulting contingency tables for each of the interview items, using net shift from initial to final interview as a measure of change in attitude (see Appendix B, Table B-12).

Just as with the participation variable, the frequency with which a parent referred to himself in the discussions influenced his attitude toward the cause of his difficulties. The greater the frequency with which

[3] Since the size of the groups varied, and since some groups were more talkative than others, each participant at each group meeting was assigned a rank according to the number of his verbal participations. The parent who participated the most was given a rank of 1, the next highest participant a rank of 2, and so forth. The ranks for each meeting were reduced proportionately to 10 ranks, since the number of parents at each meeting was not equal. A parent's "score" on this variable of participation was the average of his ranks for the meetings he attended.

a parent made a self-reference, the more likely he was to respond in the second interview that it was his own attitudes and behavior that caused his problems (Question 1-*c*). One more significant change attributable to the percentage of personal references concerned the manner in which parents accounted for their own effectiveness as parents (Question 2-*b*). This time it was parents with personal-reference scores in the two middle-range categories who changed more frequently than the other parents, more often giving their own parents in the second interview as the source from which they learned their effectiveness. The other 21 questions showed no significant differences in change of response related to personal references.

The degree of participation and frequency of personal reference were also tested for significance by using the five scales from the Parent-Attitude Survey as scores in five separate analyses of covariance. In addition to these two variables, the level of the father's education was included as a rough index of socioeconomic level. Each variable was divided into three categories, yielding a three-by-three-by-three analysis of covariance design somewhat similar to the one in Table 11.

Neither the degree of participation nor the frequency of personal reference produced differences of statistical significance.[4] The only significant difference was for the socioeconomic level on Causation, a result similar to that found earlier (Table 11).

Results for the three variables—frequency of attendance, degree of participation, and frequency of personal reference—showed these variables to have little influence on changing parental attitudes and behavior. There were occasional indications[5] that these factors tended to strengthen some of the attitudinal and behavioral changes that occurred in the Experimental Group, but the results were essentially inconclusive. It should be kept in mind, however, that the raw data used for deriving the measures of degree of participation and frequency of personal reference were rather crude; they may, indeed, be of questionable validity. In discussion

[4] To check this point further, another analysis of covariance using these same two variables, but without the level of the father's education, was computed on a larger number of subjects (216). The results were the same—no significant differences on either the single or interaction sources of variance.

[5] It should be noted that in the computation of a series of tests of significant differences on the same subjects, a significant difference at the .05 level would be expected by chance once in every 20 instances.

groups, listening may be as meaningful as talking, and the involvement of a parent in the educational process may be too complex a phenomenon to be measured accurately by simple frequency or percentage scores.

The absence of a relation between the number of meetings attended and the quantity of change in the parents was more striking, since the data on attendance were accurate. Apparently it makes little difference how many meetings a parent attends; the initial impact of the discussion method seems to be of greatest importance. In this connection, two informal observations of the groups in action may be pertinent.

The first observation concerns the reaction of the group to the nonprofessional leader. It happened in nearly every series that at the first meeting of a group the parents would attempt to put the leader in the role of an expert, even though they had been told that he was really just another parent like themselves. They would ask him questions, solicit his opinion, and in other ways treat him as though he were a specialist in the field of parent-child relations. The leader consistently declined this role, turning the questions back to the group, not giving his own opinion, and emphasizing that he was not a professional but simply another parent. At the point when the group finally accepted the fact that the leader was not an expert, there was usually a hiatus of considerable length in the conversation. Soon afterward, however, there would be an outpouring of comments and contributions by members of the group, usually on a level much more personal and emotional than that of the questions earlier addressed to the leader. Thus the shift of responsibility from leader to group (and with it an increase in the involvement of the participant) came about almost immediately. This reaction, observed over and over in the discussion groups, could be interpreted as meaning that the greatest impact of the leader occurred right at the beginning of the educational process.

The second observation concerns the frequency with which parents commented after the first meeting (or during the break for refreshments) that they were surprised to discover that so many other parents had the same problems as themselves. Strong group identification quickly developed because of commonly shared problems. This identification and the impact of the nonprofessional leader usually occurred during the first meeting the parent attended. It is conceivable, therefore, that the discussion method exerts an almost immediate effect on parents, and accounts for the surprising absence of relation between the number of meetings attended and the degree of attitudinal change.

EFFECT OF THE DISCUSSION LEADER

Although attendance, participation, and personal reference did not account for the observed changes in parental attitudes, the possibility still existed that the leader himself was an uncontrolled variable within the Experimental Group. Did some leaders inspire more change in the members of their group than other leaders? Or, to phrase the question differently, were the changes that occurred largely attributable to the leader rather than the method?

To answer this question an analysis of covariance was carried out on four concurrent discussion groups from the middle socioeconomic level, using the scores from the Parent-Attitude Survey. Each group had a different leader. Two of the leaders were men, one experienced and the other serving as a leader for the first time. Of the two women, one was experienced and the other was a novice at leading group discussions.

None of the differences among the four leaders was significant on any of the five attitude scales. These results indicate that the leader himself was not an important variable in the quantity of change that occurred in the parents. These findings leave the discussion method *per se* as the most likely explanation for the differences obtained among the research categories.

The principal hypothesis concerning parents was clearly confirmed: discussion-group parents did show significantly greater changes in reported attitudes and behavior than did parents in any of the control groups. Results for the secondary hypotheses—concerning the effects of attendance, participation, and personal reference on the quantity of attitude change—were equivocal. While the data indicated that these three variables did strengthen some of the changes that occurred in the discussion-group parents, for the most part the results were negative. A small study of the leader as a variable revealed that the observed changes in the discussion groups were attributable to the discussion method, not to the individual leader.

FINDINGS CONCERNING CHILDREN

The principal hypothesis of the research design was applicable to children as well as to parents. Did children in the Experimental Group change significantly more than children in the control groups as a result of their parents' attendance at the discussion meetings? The children's data provided an unusually rigorous test of the effectiveness of the discussion technique, since the behavior of the child in school was quite far removed from the educational method under investigation. Change in the child's behavior was dependent on a sequence of steps beginning with change in his parent's attitudes. It bears repeating that none of the children in any of the groups attended any program themselves.

The two measures of child behavior used as dependent variables were the sociometric evaluation based on peer-group selections and the teacher ratings. These data from children were tested for significance by analysis of covariance, using the same four independent variables as in the Parent-Attitude Survey study: research category (five intervals); socioeconomic level (three intervals of the father's education); age of child (two intervals); and sex of the child (two intervals). The results of this analysis are summarized in Table 12.

The predictions in Hypothesis I concerning the value of the discussion method with parents for improving the behavior of their children were confirmed by the sociometric data; that is, children of parents who attended discussion meetings improved significantly more than did children of control-group parents, in the degree of acceptance such children received from their classmates. The quantity of change for each of the four research groups is illustrated in Figure 43.[6] These means show definite improvement in the sociometric standing for the children of discussion-group parents, while that of the children of all the control groups remains unchanged. These results can be interpreted in terms of the hypothetical schema presented in Chapter V. The attitudinal and behavioral changes that occurred in parents who attended the discussion groups influenced the parent-child relation to the extent that the child was able to improve his classmate relations at school. None of the remaining three independent variables or higher order interactions proved significant for the sociometric data.

The teachers' ratings of children, on the other hand, revealed no significant differences among the research categories. Table 12 reveals, however, that two other sources of variation reached a significant level of probability—the sex of the child and the interaction between the sex and the age of the child. The group means indicate that girls tended to im-

[6] Since the two subdivisions by attendance in the Experimental Group had almost exactly the same means, they are combined in Figure 43.

FIGURE 43

Initial and Final Means on the Sociometric Evaluation for the Children of Parents in the Research Groups

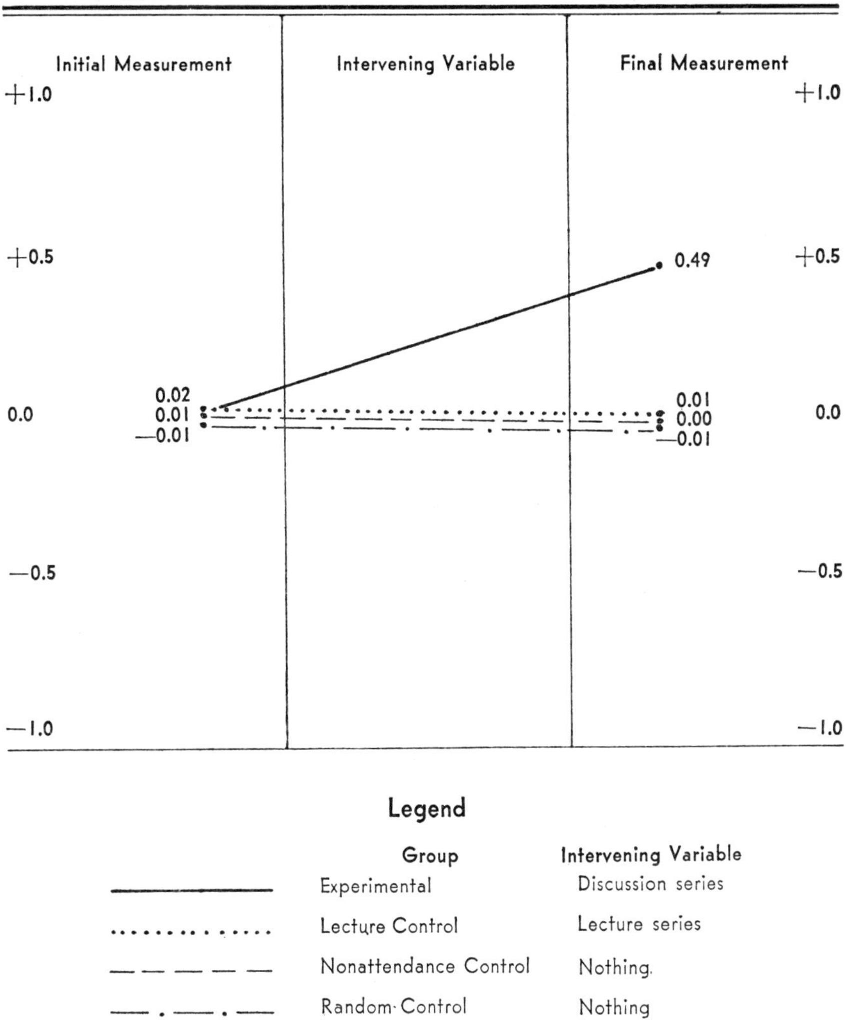

TABLE 12

Analysis of Covariance for Research Category, Socioeconomic Level, Age of Child, and Sex of Child, Using the Sociometric Evaluation and Teacher Ratings as Dependent Variables

Source of Variation	Degrees of Freedom	Sociometric Evaluation F[1]	p	Teacher Ratings F[1]	p
A Research category	4	5.34	.001	1.18	. .
B Socioeconomic level	2	2.25	. .		
C Age of child	1	3.57	. .		
D Sex of child	1			6.83	.01
AB interaction	8			1.46	. .
AC interaction	4				
AD interaction	4	1.42	. .		
BC interaction	2	3.27	. .		
BD interaction	2	2.40	. .		
CD interaction	1			5.87	.05
ABC interaction	8				
ABD interaction	8				
BCD interaction	2			1.21	. .
ACD interaction	4				
ABCD interaction	8				

[1] F-ratios less than 1.0 have been omitted.

prove and boys did not, as judged by their teachers. The age-sex interaction revealed that younger girls showed more positive change than older girls, while neither age groups of boys showed any change. These results indicate that teachers were more likely to see improvement in girls than in boys, just as they had rated girls significantly higher than boys on the initial measurement. A possible explanation for this strong sex difference in favor of girls is that, with very few exceptions, the teachers who made the ratings were women, and may have had a tendency to view girls more positively than boys.

SUMMARY OF FINDINGS

The research design, the measurements, and the statistical analysis of the data were designed to test the effectiveness of the discussion method. The main results are:

1. Parents who attended the discussion-group series *did* show positive changes in their attitudes as measured by the Parent-Attitude Survey.

These changes were significantly greater than those of parents in the three control groups.

2. Parents who attended the discussion groups also changed their attitudes and behavior as shown by responses to the Parent Interview, again significantly more than parents in the control groups.

3. Children of parents who attended the discussion meetings improved in their classmate relations significantly more than did the children of parents in the control groups, but not in their ratings by teachers, even though none of the children participated in the program. The observed changes in the attitudes and behavior of discussion-group parents were apparently strong and pervasive enough to influence the social acceptance of their children by classmates.

4. The number of discussion meetings attended, the amount of verbal participation in the discussion, and the frequency of personal references generally proved to be unrelated to the quantity of attitudinal and behavioral change in the parents. Nor did the individual nonprofessional leader prove to be a factor of any importance, giving rise to the conclusion that the discussion method *per se*, not the leader, is the crucial element involved.

On the basis of these results, we concluded that the discussion-group method is a powerful educational technique for changing attitudes and behavior.

XI

Implications of This Study for Adult Education

THE UNDERLYING ASSUMPTION OF THE GROUP-DISCUSSION method used in this Project was that the responsibility for the educational process must rest with the learner. This responsibility included his supplying the content of the program as well as deciding upon the manner in which the content was treated. No plan of study, no agenda, no textbook was used. Parents were free to discuss any topic that was of concern to them so long as it fell within the broad area of parent-child relations. By sharing experiences and thoughts, members of the group reached their own solutions for the problems they discussed, and each parent was free to accept or reject what was offered in the group, to pick and choose as he pleased among the ideas presented.

This atmosphere of freedom and shared responsibility fostered a feeling of "belonging" on the part of the group members. No one was "in charge." There was no expert or consultant on whom the group could rely; even the discussion leader was on the same footing as everyone else. What the group was, how it functioned, and what it accomplished was due to its members. The individual parent felt that the group was genuinely his, and the process of group identification was thereby facilitated.

Through this process and by sharing the responsibility for the group the individual participant had the opportunity to become personally involved in the educational method. He could express his hopes and fears, discuss his worries, and relate his experiences to a group that was interested and sympathetic because all its members were in the same situation. He also had the opportunity to participate in the experiences, problems, and ideas of others, to agree or disagree, to empathize, to share feelings and emotions. This method of education was not objective, but rather something that was *felt*—lived through at an emotional level. The learner became involved emotionally as well as intellectually, a necessary condition if changes in attitude and behavior are to occur.

Another underlying assumption was implicit in this method: parents can learn from each other. Many parents do not need the counsel of experts or more information about parent-child relations. They either possess an adequate fund of information or can obtain it. What they lack is the ability to put into effective use what they already know, that is, they need to know how to utilize more fully their existing capacities for parenthood. The discussion method gave the parent an opportunity for self-growth and the development of his potentials in the manner that was appropriate for him as an individual. It did not attempt directly to teach him to be a "good" parent.

POSSIBILITIES FOR FUTURE RESEARCH

The effectiveness of this method of group discussion in bringing about changes in parental attitude and behavior was clearly demonstrated by the results of the research. These results did not show, however, precisely *how* the changes were brought about. There was no systematic analysis of the process. The evaluation was an external one. Parents were tested for attitudes and behavior before and after their participation in the group discussions, but not during it. Although the method was proved effective, still further improvement might be achieved through a better understanding of how it functions. Additional research is therefore needed to throw light on the ways in which this kind of discussion method works and through what mechanisms the attitudinal changes occur. Such questions as how much influence the stimulus material had on the process remain unanswered, although the indications are that this influence is relatively slight. Are there other stimuli that would serve better than films for this purpose? Is any stimulus at all necessary? Some experimentation with the use of plays, tape recordings, role-playing, and lectures as stimulus material was done in the course of the Project, but it was not systematically evaluated.

Another area for future research concerns the durableness of changes brought about by the discussion method. Are these changes permanent modifications of parental attitudes and behavior, or will these parents revert in time to their old patterns? We attempted to follow up as well as to provide repeated exposure to the method by holding group-discussion series in the same school for four consecutive years. These repeated discussion groups were successful in terms of attendance, but the research effort failed for lack of sufficient data, since the rejection rate for interview appointments by parents who had participated in interviews twice before was prohibitively high. With better control of subjects, however, such a study could perhaps be carried out.

The nonprofessional leader himself is also a promising area for investigation. It seems clear that he is the crux of this group-discussion method. The fact that he is not a professional eliminates the inhibitory influence that an expert automatically exerts on a group, for it is not his function to control or take responsibility for the group. His position in this regard is no different from that of any of the other parents. The nonprofessional leader enhances the opportunity for individual involvement by providing an atmosphere of acceptance, giving everyone an opportunity to talk, summarizing, rephrasing and clarifying, or breaking up subgroups; but he does *not* insert his own opinions, provide solutions, or give suggestions or advice. To this extent the word "leader" is a misnomer; the leader in this discussion method is actually a moderator.

The remarkable impact that a nonprofessional leader has on a group was observed during the study, but not investigated. Our attempt to study the leaders by psychological evaluations was not completed because of their resistance to the measuring instruments. Nevertheless, these difficulties are surmountable; and research studies on the leader, his selection and training, and his effect on the discussion process would be particularly valuable, for he appears to be the key to the uniqueness of this method.

GENERAL APPLICATIONS

Although gaps remain in the research and some important angles of the discussion method were not investigated, the fundamental question concerning the value of the method in the area of parent-child relations was clearly answered. The discussion-group method, as used in this

Project, was highly effective in changing parents' attitudes and behavior. It must be kept in mind, however, that the first requirement for the success of the method is that it be feasible for the setting in which it is to be used. While the results of the research itself are not to be minimized, the current demonstration that this method can be successfully carried out in an ordinary community is perhaps of equal importance.

The feasibility of the discussion method was shown by four years of successful use in Austin, and was further demonstrated by the fact that the community has continued the program after the Research Project has been completed. The program was acceptable to organizations in the community that were concerned with educating men and women for parenthood, and they made it possible for us to use their existing facilities and organizational framework. Undoubtedly the acceptability of this method to these community groups contributed heavily to its success. Not only did these organizations oil the mechanics of carrying out the program, but their sponsorship placed the program within the activities of the community itself. The educational effort was something done by the people in the community, not a program imposed from the outside. Community support is essential if this type of educational program is to succeed.

The fact that the discussion method does not rely on professionals, except to train the leaders, greatly increased its usefulness. Any plan that calls for employing professionals for an extensive program of group education is clearly beyond the financial means of most communities, even if enough professionals are available. The use of volunteers and existing physical facilities made the cost of this particular program relatively low. Once the leaders were trained, the only expenses were for the publicity, refreshments, child care, and (sometimes) custodian's fees. The workshops for training leaders did demand the services of professionals and therefore were more expensive than the discussion groups. Each workshop produced many leaders, however, who in turn worked with many parents. Thus the cost of the workshop encompassed many participants in the educational program, making the unit cost per parent very low.

Another point of major significance regarding the usefulness of this method is that it worked equally well at all socioeconomic levels. The analysis of the initial measurements in this study demonstrates the strong influence which the socioeconomic level exerts on parental attitudes. An educational program aimed at the middle-class parent is, therefore, certain to miss the mark at the lower levels. In the group-discussion method the parents themselves not only determine the content of the program according to their own needs and interests, but they also discuss these subjects in their own language and within their own frame of reference. Consequently, the twin problems of appropriateness of content and communication across social classes become nonexistent with this method. The same advantage holds for ethnic groups in the community as well. Some of the most animated and best-attended groups of the entire Project were those held in the Negro schools. In one of the school districts with a high percentage of Latin-American families it was more effectual to hold the discussion in Spanish, a departure demonstrating a degree of flexibility inherent in the discussion technique that is not possible in most of the other educational methods.

It should be emphasized that this method was used in the present study for educational, not therapeutic, purposes. The parents who participated were essentially in the normal personality range, with everyday problems and concerns. The one instance in which a discussion series failed involved a group of parents whose problems appeared to be at a clinical level of severity. Accomplishing change in attitudes and behavior was the primary goal of the educational part of this Research Project, a goal that is not universally shared by all forms of group education. Where an increase in skill or information is of primary importance, group discussion without an expert would hardly be the method to choose. Similarly, the informal, loose structure of these discussion groups is probably unsuitable for groups faced with the responsibility of making decisions. In short, the fact that this method proved highly successful in fulfilling the purposes for which it was particularly designed does not give it universal applicability.

On the other hand, there is no reason to assume that parent-child relations is the only area in which the method would be practicable. Although they were not included in the research design, discussion series were held during the course of the Project in such diverse areas as problems peculiar to the military family, to the three-generation family, and to Civil Defense. While there was no formal evaluation of the effectiveness of these projects, the discussion method appeared to work as fruitfully with them as with the groups concerned with parent-child relations.

Criteria for determining the suitability of this method in other situations should take into consideration both the content and the goals of the proposed program. If the topic of discussion is one in which feelings and emotions are important, and if the goal is attitudinal change and personal development, the discussion method merits serious consideration. If, on the other hand, the aim of the program is to acquire knowledge or skill, or if the content is largely academic or intellectual, then a more traditional method will probably serve better.

Many of the nonprofessional leaders who served in the Project carried over their skills to other community organizations to which they belonged. The group-discussion method was used in such programs as those initiated by churches, civic organizations, clubs, or schools. The relatively small cost of the method and its popularity with the participants are strong inducements for an organization considering an educational program. Smaller communities, where professionals may be entirely lacking, could bring in a consultant to train the leaders and then carry out the program independently.

Teachers, employees, the aged—nearly any group in which attitudes are important could profitably participate in group discussions. Students, for instance, seem to offer a fertile field for mental health education by the group-discussion method, with dormitory facilities and student organizations providing a ready-made vehicle to carry out the program. Other specific groups include families of mental patients, alcoholics, or retarded children. Possibly the method could be used successfully with groups of people who face more severe problems—terminal-cancer patients and inmates of prisons might respond favorably to this type of education. In any of these applications it is essential that members of the group be in a similar situation or face the same problems, that nonprofessional leaders be recruited from within the group, and that the goal of the program be concerned with attitudes and their modification.

Group discussions led by a nonprofessional leader, let it be said once more, proved to be a powerful method for changing attitudes and behavior in the area of parent-child relations. The low cost of this method, its ready acceptance by participants, and its flexibility make its use as limitless as the ingenuity of the organizer of educational programs.

APPENDIX A

The Measuring Instruments

PARENT-ATTITUDE SURVEY

INSTRUCTIONS

On the following pages are a number of statements regarding parents and children. Please indicate your agreement or disagreement with each statement in the following manner:

Strongly Agree ——cross out letter "A" on answer sheet
Agree ——cross out letter "a" on answer sheet
Undecided ——cross out letter "u" on answer sheet
Disagree ——cross out letter "d" on answer sheet
Strongly Disagree——cross out letter "D" on answer sheet

For example: if you *strongly agree* with the following statement, you would mark it in this way:

Boys are more active than girls. ~~A~~ a u d D

All your answers are to be marked on the green answer sheet. As you turn each page, the next column of answers will appear. Please do not write on this page or on the statements.

This survey is concerned only with the attitudes and opinions that parents have; there are no "right" or "wrong" answers. Work just as rapidly as you can—it is your first impression that we are interested in. There is no time limit.

REMEMBER . . . . A = Strongly Agree
a = Agree
u = Undecided
d = Disagree
D = Strongly Disagree

Please turn the page and go ahead . . . .

NOTE. The items used in the Parent-Attitude Survey are listed in Chapter VI, Tables 1–5.

LETTER TO PARENTS

PARENT-CHILD RELATIONS PROJECT

CARL F. HEREFORD, PH.D.
RESEARCH DIRECTOR

2410 SAN ANTONIO STREET
AUSTIN 5, TEXAS
PHONE GREENWOOD 2-2587

Dear Parent:

As one part of a project concerning parent-child relations, we are interviewing parents in several elementary-school districts in Austin. The project is financed by the Hogg Foundation of the University of Texas. Since you are the parent of an elementary-school child, we would like very much to send an interviewer to your home to talk with you for about an hour regarding your attitudes and opinions on parent-child relations.

Your name, of course, will not appear on your replies to our questions, as we are only interested in gaining an over-all view from several hundred parents. We will be asking other parents in your school to cooperate with us also, as well as parents in other school districts. There will be a follow-up interview with all parents in about two or three months.

The interview does not contain any embarrassing questions and you will find our interviewer courteous and friendly. Your participation is wholly voluntary and we will try to take as little of your time as possible. We will contact you in the near future regarding an appointment for the interview. In the meantime, if you have any questions, please feel free to call the number given above.

Thank you very much,

Carl F. Hereford

Carl F. Hereford, Ph.D.
Project Director

CFH/me

P.S. Here are some questions parents have asked us in the past, and the answers:

"Are you selling anything?" "No."

"What are you going to do with all this material?" "The results of the entire project will eventually be submitted to scientific publications."

"Why was I selected? Why are my attitudes important?" "Because you have an elementary-age school child."

"Does this have anything to do with the PTA Study Group?" "We are interviewing in the same school districts where the PTA program is in progress, but whether or not a parent participates in the PTA does not make any difference."

INSTRUCTIONS FOR INTERVIEWERS

(Initial Interview)

General:

The interviewer should introduce himself as being from the Parent-Child Relations Project and refer to the appointment that was set up by telephone. If parent wants more information regarding sponsorship, he can be told that the Project is sponsored by the local Mental Health Society and the Hogg Foundation of the University of Texas.

If parent wonders how his name was selected, he can be told that we are choosing parents with children enrolled in elementary schools and that we are also working in other schools. If parent asks if he was chosen because he signed up for the Study Group, he should be told that we are trying to get as many parents as possible, including those who did not sign up, but that we are interested in getting as many people who signed up for the program as possible.

Throughout the interview, caution should be taken not to offend or disturb the parent. It is preferable to drop a question, or even an entire area, rather than to cause ill will.

Sequence of Interview

The green sheet should be filled out before the interview commences or after it is over. Do not ask the parent about the items on the green sheet! These are rated on the basis of the interviewer's observations. The white sheets contain the questions to be asked and the identification material should be obtained first. When the interview has been completed, the parent is given the Attitude Scale. This is essentially self-administering but the interviewer should check to see that the parent understands the directions and is marking the answer sheet correctly. While the parent is completing the Attitude Scale, the interviewer should check over his interview and may wish to ask the parent for clarification on certain points after he has completed the Attitude Scale.

When everything has been completed, the parent should be asked if he will be willing to participate in an interview again in two or three months. If the parent agrees, make a note of this on the identification sheet.

INSTRUCTIONS FOR INTERVIEWERS

(Final Interview)

General:

The interviewer should introduce himself as being from the Parent-Child Relations Project and refer to the appointment that was set up by telephone. If parent wants more information regarding sponsorship, he can be told that the Project is sponsored by the local Mental Health Society and the Hogg Foundation of the University of Texas.

Explain to parent that this re-interview is to see if there have been any changes since the first interview. Ask the parent to answer the questions the way he feels right now, and not to be concerned if this is not the same answer given previously. Point out that some of the questions will be the same as before, some will be different. If parent complains about the repetition (either on the interview or on the Attitude Scale) explain that this is common practice in research studies, and that even if the parent feels there have been no changes, it is important to answer the questions again. Be careful to avoid the impression that we are "checking up" on the parent's accuracy or consistency.

Throughout the interview, caution should be taken not to offend or disturb the parent. It is preferable to drop a question, or even an entire area, rather than to cause ill will.

Sequence of Interview

The green sheet should be filled out before the interview commences or after it is over. Do not ask the parent about the items on the green sheet. These are rated on the basis of the interviewers' observations. The white sheets contain the questions to be asked and the identification material should be obtained first. When the interview has been completed, the parent is given the Attitude Scale. This is essentially self-administering but the interviewer should check to see that the parent understands the directions and is marking the answer sheet correctly. While the parent is completing the Attitude Scale, the interviewer should check over his interview and may wish to ask the parent for clarification on certain points after he has completed the Attitude Scale.

When everything has been completed, thank the parent for his cooperation. If parent asks about results of the study, explain that it will not be completed until parents from many more schools have been interviewed, probably another year or two.

NEIGHBORHOOD AND HOME-RATING SHEET

Address:____

Neighborhood

Residential ( ) Business ( ) Industrial ( ) Suburban ( ) Farm ( )

Traffic: Heavy ( ) Medium ( ) Light ( )

Dwelling Units: Crowded ( ) Well-spaced ( ) Distant ( )

Play space for children: Ample ( ) Some ( ) None ( )

Condition of neighborhood Good ( ) Average ( ) Run-down ( )

The Home

House ( ) Apartment ( ) Duplex ( ) Farm ( ) Other:____________

Living space: Crowded ( ) Comfortable ( ) Spacious ( )

Condition of home: Well-kept ( ) Average ( ) Run-down ( )

How would you estimate the home compares with others in the neighborhood?

Better________

About the same________

In worse condition________

Comments, if any:

Interview by ________________________

Date ________________________

IDENTIFICATION

Children:

Name	Age	Sex	Grade	Teacher	School

Mother: Age____ Education:__________ Occupation:__________

Father: Age:____ Education:__________ Occupation:__________

Religious Affiliation: Protestant______
Catholic______
Jewish______
Other______

Church Attendance: Regular______
Occasional______
Seldom______

Available for re-interview ____________________

Comment____________________

INTERVIEW QUESTIONS

(for Use of Interviewers Only)

1. All parents have some difficulties in raising children. In general, what has been the hardest thing about child-rearing for you?

   a. What have you done to help this situation?

   b. How has this worked out?

   c. [If nothing on causation.][1] What do you think caused this situation to develop?

   d. How common are situations like this with other parents and children you know?

   e. Have you ever sought outside help in this matter? [Talked it over with a friend, physician, guidance center, teacher, etc.]

   f. How did this work out?

2. A parent is expected to do many things—and make many decisions—as a part of the job of raising children. Some of these things are fun, some are not so much fun. As you think about it, what are the things that please you most about being a parent? [What advantages do you have over a person without children?]

   a. [If not already answered.] In what way do you feel that you are most effective as a parent? [In what way are you best as a parent?]

   b. How do you account for this? [Any other causes?] [What made you this way?]

3. What are the things that worry you most about being a parent? [What worries do you have that a person without children wouldn't have?]

   a. What brings them [these things] about [causes them to happen]?

   b. [If not already answered.] In what way do you feel most ineffective as a parent? [In what way are you worst as a parent?]

   c. How do you account for this [ineffectiveness]?

[1] The skeletal material in brackets was intended to aid the interviewer by suggesting to him ramifications of the question that would elicit more information from the parents.

4. Sometimes it's hard to know just where to draw the line with children. How much freedom do you allow your children? [Strict? Lenient? Flexible?]

    a. Can you give some examples? [Activities, responsibility for school, allowance, choice of playmates, etc.]
    b. How do other families in the neighborhood handle situations like this?
    c. Are there some children you would prefer he or she didn't play with? [If so, why?]
    d. How does he or she feel about this?

5. Sometimes it's necessary to punish a child. What method of punishment do you usually use?

    a. Any others [if necessary]?
    b. What kinds of things do you usually have to punish your child for?
    c. How do these methods work?
    d. How often do you have to punish your child?

6. Most all families have trouble getting along from time to time. Where does the trouble usually occur in your family?

    a. [If not already answered.] What members of the family are most often involved [or cause the trouble]?
    b. [If not already answered.] What kinds of situations seem to cause the most trouble in your family?
    c. Is there anyone outside the family that regularly has much to do with the care and upbringing of the children? [If so, who?]
    d. Does this relation ever cause any problems? [If answer is yes, ask how or what kind.]

7. None of us are perfect, of course, and neither are our children. But what do you consider to be the ideal characteristics of an elementary-school age child? [Most desirable qualities, the "perfect" child.]

    a. What about behavior [if not already mentioned]?
    b. What about getting along with others [if not already mentioned]?
    c. What about relation with parents [if not already mentioned]?
    d. What do you think are the most important characteristics a person should have to be a good parent?

INSTRUCTIONS FOR INTERVIEW CODERS

The basic procedure is to read the response to each question to be coded, decide which category of the Interview Code for that question fits the response best, and then enter the number of that category in the proper column or columns of the Data Sheet. Code for content only, i.e., what the parent said. Do not make inferences or evaluations, though interpretations of the responses may be necessary. Note that some questions are coded more than once. The first response is the one given first, not necessarily the most important one. Note also that some questions are coded together—in which case the information coded may be in response to any of the questions in that combination. Code only the number of responses called for, even though more may be present.

In general, consider only the responses to the question or questions being coded, though sometimes responses to other questions on the same page may be used to clarify the response being considered. In any event, do not take into account responses from pages other than the one on which you are working.

Begin with Question 1 after entering the identification number (in red on card). Do not read the preliminary pages before Question 1.

The interviews are grouped in blocks of 25, with one Data Sheet for each block. Complete each block before beginning another, and keep the interviews in order within each block. Each Data Sheet must have a number in each square (no blanks), and only one number in each square. Do not write the code numbers on the interview itself, just on the data sheet. Be sure your numbers are clear and legible.

Interjudge reliability is very important. Make sure you understand the meaning of the code, and if you are in doubt, ask. Inconsistencies among raters are very difficult to handle statistically. While it is of course undesirable to lose data, don't hesitate to use the zero category for uncodable responses. From the point of view of statistical analysis, zero codes may mean lost data, but they cannot mean incorrect data.

The interviews were conducted with the clear understanding that the information obtained was completely confidential and was to be used for research purposes only. Identification material is on the interview. Please help us keep our pledge of confidentiality.

INTERVIEW CODE

Identification: Copy identification number from interview exactly

Code

Question 1. Difficulties in raising children

Code	Category	Item
00	No information, or not covered by code	
01	Discipline—minding, obeying, making child do something, etc.	
02	Sibling rivalry, problems between children	
03	Normal adjustment or developmental problems	Interpersonal—getting along with others
04		Responsibility
05		Passivity—shy, won't fight back
06		Aggressiveness—rowdy, noisy
07		Dawdling
08		Other
09	Specific symptoms	Thumbsucking
10		Wetting or soiling
11		Eating problems
12		Nailbiting
13		Withdrawal, extreme shyness
14		Extreme destructiveness or aggression
15		Phobias or fears
16		Other
17	Physical health or illness, safety	
18	Financial	
19	Problem within parent	Inadequacy
20		Indecision
21		Inconsistency between parents
22		Lack of patience
23		Other
24	States that he has no problem	

Question1-*a*. How problem handled

Code	Category	Item
0	No information, or not covered by code	
1	Punishment	Corporal—spankings, beatings, etc.
2		Noncorporal—withdrawal of privileges, etc.
3		Not specified
4	Rewards, inducements, bribes, prizes	
5	Discussed with child, explained, reasoned, lectured, etc.	
6	Manipulated environment in some manner	
7	Changed own behavior or attitude	
8	Sought outside help of any nature or kind	
9	Has done nothing	

Code

Question 1-*b*. How solution worked out

0 No information, or not covered by code
1 Made matters worse
2 No change
3 Slight improvement
4 Improvement
5 Great improvement

Question 1-*c*. Causation

0 No information, or not covered by code
1 Inherited
2 Inherent characteristic of child or children in general
3 Physical or health
4 Age relation—oldest, youngest, close together, only child, etc.
5 Normal development or growth—"stages," etc.
6 Environmental situation
7 Culture, society—"changing times," etc.
8 Parent's behavior or attitudes
9 Does not know

Question1-*d*. Commonness of problem

0 No information, or not covered by code
1 Unusual, unique, special situation
2 Occasional, but not unusual
3 Common, or fairly common
4 Very common, quite common
5 Present in all families, universal, widespread

Question 1-*e*. Outside help for solving problem

0 No information, or not covered by code
1 No outside help
2 Mother of parent
3 Member of family (other than mother) or relative
4 Friend or neighbor
5 Teacher or other school personnel
6 Physician
7 Individual specialist or practitioner other than physician
8 Professional agency (Guidance Center, Family Service, etc.)
9 Yes (not specified)

Question 1-*f*. Effectiveness of outside help

0 No information, or not covered by code
1 Negative evaluation
2 Neutral evaluation
3 Positive evaluation

Code

Question 2. What parents like about parenthood

0 No information, or not covered by code
1 Companionship
2 Receiving love and affection from child
3 Achievement by the child—growing up, development, learning

4	Meeting child's needs, giving to child	Affection or emotional
5		Education, learning
6		Physical, health, cleanliness
7		General or not specified

8 Interesting, meaningful experience, important job
9 Help or contribution from child

Question 2-*a*. Parental effectiveness

0 No information, or not covered by code
1 Guidance, direction, teaching

2	Providing for, taking care of child	Physical—food, shelter, clothing, etc.
3		Emotional—security, love, etc.
4		Spiritual—church, religion, etc.
5		Other, or not specified

6 Supervision, discipline, control
7 Participation with child, sharing activities, companionship
8 Don't know
9 Not effective

Question 2-*b*. How account for effectiveness

0 No information, or not covered by code
1 Experience, practice
2 Learned from own parents, own childhood
3 Learned from sources other than own parents or childhood
4 Love, maternal feeling, interest
5 Don't know, just am, just happened

Question 3. Parental worries

00 No information, or not covered by code
01 Behavior of child—obedience, manners, quarreling, selfishness, etc.
02 How child will "turn out," outcome
03 Character development
04 Education, school grades
05 Physical—illness, accidents, injuries
06 Finances
07 Separation—leaving child alone, when child is away from home
08 Activities of child
09 Adolescence, teen-age problems
10 Specific symptoms—nervousness, nailbiting, wetting, etc.
11 Unwholesome or undesirable influences
12 Sex education
13 Religious or spiritual
14 Environmental situations—moving, father's job, etc.
15 Own adequacy
16 Nothing, no worries
17 Broken home—separation or divorce

Code

Omit Question 3-*a*

Question 3-*b*. Parental ineffectiveness

0 No information, or not covered by code
1 Impatience, lose temper, cross, lack of patience, etc.
2 Not enough time, too busy, too many outside activities
3 Discipline—too lenient, too strict, can't make child mind
4 Inconsistency
5 Lack of closeness, can't "talk to" or "reach" child
6 Lack of knowledge, education
7 Nervousness, easily upset
8 Doesn't feel ineffective

Omit Question 3-*c*

Question 4. Amount of freedom

0 No information, or not covered by code
1 Very strict
2 Moderately strict
3 Average, about the same as others
4 Moderate amount of freedom
5 Lots of freedom
6 Varies with situation

Omit Questions 4-*a* and 4-*b*

Question 4-*c*. Parental restrictions on playmates

0 No information, or not covered by code
1 Yes
2 No

Omit Question 4-*d*

Questions 5 and 5-*a*. Methods of punishment

0 No information, or not covered by code

1	Corporal punishment	Spanking, beating, whipping
2		Use of paddle, belt, switch, etc.
3		Other

4 Withdrawal of privileges, TV, cookies, etc.
5 Confinement—send to room, to bed, sit in chair, can't go out, etc.
6 Verbal—talk to, lecture, threaten
7 Does not punish

Code

Question 5-*b*. What parents punish for

0 No information, or not covered by code
1 Disobedience, not minding, not doing as told
2 Unfairness, unkindness
3 Lying, telling stories, untruthful
4 Carelessness, forgetting, lack of attention, thoughtlessness
5 Insolence, talking back, sassy
6 Aggressiveness, fighting, fussing, quarreling
7 Does not need punishment

Question 5-*c*. How well punishment works

0 No information, or not covered by code
1 Not effective
2 Effective (qualified)
3 Very effective, effective

Omit Question 5-*d*

Questions 6 and 6-*b*. Family troubles

0 No information, or not covered by code
1 Behavior of child or children
2 Getting ready to go out, going to bed, dawdling
3 Family agreement on activities, where to go, etc.
4 Differences in age of children
5 Physical or health
6 Parental disagreements
7 Lack of time, rushed, long working hours, not home enough
8 Finances
9 No troubles

Question 6-*a*. Who involved

0 No information, or not covered by code
1 Child or children
2 Mother
3 Father
4 Parents
5 All family
6 Others, relatives
7 Others, not relatives

Question 6-*c*. Outsiders for child care

0 No information, or not covered by code
1 No
2 Yes (unspecified)
3 Grandparent or grandparents
4 Relative other than grandparent
5 Unrelated individual—neighbor, friend
6 Agency, school, child-care center, etc.

Code

Question 6-*d*. Problems caused by outsiders

0 No information, or not covered by code
1 No
2 Yes
3 Equivocal

Questions 7, 7-*a*, 7-*b*, 7-*c*. Ideal child

00 No information, or not covered by code
01 Good interpersonal relations—gets along with others, friendly, sociable, cooperative, likes others
02 Obedience, well-behaved
03 Compassion, understanding, kind, considerate
04 Intelligent, smart, educational effort and achievement
05 Emotionally well-adjusted
06 Respect for parents, elders, authority
07 Honesty, fairness, truthfulness
08 Independent, dependable, self-reliant, responsible
09 Assertive—stands up for self, says what he thinks
10 Appearance, grooming, neatness, cleanliness
11 Punctuality
12 Physically well, healthy
13 Don't know
14 Happy, contented

Question 7-*d*. Ideal parent

00 No information, or not covered by code
01 Understanding
02 Patience
03 Honesty
04 Love children, like them, want them, interest in them
05 Moral values, religious, spiritual, right and wrong
06 Tolerance, broad-minded, open-minded
07 Perseverance, fortitude, emotional strength
08 Well-adjusted, good or sound personality
09 Sense of humor
10 Consistency
11 Physically well, healthy
12 Set a good example
13 Don't know

LETTER TO TEACHERS (INITIAL MEASUREMENT)

PARENT-CHILD RELATIONS PROJECT

CARL F. HEREFORD, PH.D.
RESEARCH DIRECTOR

2410 SAN ANTONIO STREET
AUSTIN 5, TEXAS
PHONE GREENWOOD 2-2587

Dear Teacher:

Thank you very much for your cooperation with our sociometric work with your class a few days ago. Now we would like to ask your cooperation again, this time on a brief teacher rating, the materials and instructions for which are enclosed.

As a teacher, you are able to supply information that is not available anywhere else regarding children's behavior. This information is essential to us in our project in Parent-Child Relations. The information you give us is, of course, completely confidential. It will not be used with parents or become a part of school records. As a matter of fact, we are not interested in individual children but only in groups. We do not even keep a permanent record of the individual child's name--the information you give us will be transferred to a code system.

Many teachers asked for a report of the sociometric techniques we used in your classroom. We will be happy to send you a report of our work in your class. However, since we plan to be back in your school within the next two or three months to do some more evaluations, it would be better for us and would make the report more meaningful to you if we wait until then to prepare the report.

Thank you again for your cooperation. Since it is highly desirable for all of the teacher ratings to be done at approximately the same time, we would appreciate it if you would complete your rating in the next day or two. It should not take more than fifteen or twenty minutes. Any comments or suggestions you might have regarding our work would be greatly appreciated.

Sincerely,

Carl F. Hereford

Carl F. Hereford, Ph.D., Director
Parent-Child Relations Project

CFH/me
encls.

LETTER TO TEACHERS (FINAL MEASUREMENT)

PARENT-CHILD RELATIONS PROJECT

CARL F. HEREFORD, PH.D.
RESEARCH DIRECTOR

1101 WEST 40TH
AUSTIN 5, TEXAS
PHONE GLENDALE 3-1331

Dear Teacher:

We would again like to ask your cooperation in connection with our sociometric work with your class. This is our second visit with your class and it is desirable to have a second teacher rating, made in the same manner as before. We are enclosing the instructions and name cards just as in the first teacher rating you made.

Since it is desirable that all the teacher ratings be done at approximately the same time, we ask that you please complete this second rating within the next day or two.

As we told you before, the information you furnish us will be held in strict confidence and a report of our work with your class will be sent to you as soon as we can complete the necessary work.

Again, thank you very much for your cooperation.

Sincerely,

Carl F. Hereford

Carl F. Hereford, Ph.D., Director
Parent-Child Relations Project

CFH/me
encls.

TEACHER RATINGS
INSTRUCTIONS

Materials

Stack of name cards, each bearing the name of one child in your class.
Nine small envelopes, each with a Roman and an Arabic numeral.

First

Spread out the nine envelopes left to right, according to the *Roman* numerals, I on the left and IX on the right. The Roman numeral on the envelope corresponds to the rank (I is highest or best, IX is lowest or poorest). The Arabic numeral represents the number of name cards to be placed in each rank (necessary for statistical purposes).

You are now ready to rank the children in your class according to their

ADJUSTMENT TO THE CLASSROOM SETTING

The particular factors that we have in mind as far as classroom adjustment is concerned are:

The child's relation with you, the teacher.
How well he is accepted by the other children.
His reaction to rules and regulations.
His attitude and cooperativeness.
His general emotional maturity.

We are *not* directly interested in the child's academic achievement or his intelligence level. Neither are we interested in the social or economic status of his family. The kind of adjustment problem a child may have does not concern us either. For example, a very withdrawn child and a very aggressive child might both receive the same low ranking.

Second

Sort the name cards now into appropriate ranks, comparing one child with the others. The child with the best over-all adjustment goes in Rank I, the one with the poorest in Rank IX, and the others distributed in between. The *Arabic* numeral on each envelope tells you the number of cards that must go in each rank. The ranks are relative, of course, and apply only to this group of children. It is a good idea to make the sort fairly quickly, as your first impressions are usually accurate. It is frequently easier to start by singling out the children at the extreme ends of the rankings. It is also helpful to lay the cards out in such a manner that all are visible (not stacked one on another). This facilitates comparing one child with another.

Third

When the sort is completed:

1. Check to be sure you have the right number of cards in each pile, according to the Arabic numeral on the envelope. If any adjustments have to be made (i.e., not enough or too many cards) make the adjustment in the middle rank, Rank V).
2. Place each pile of cards in its envelope. *Please do not seal the envelopes,* as they will be used again.
3. Place the small envelopes in the large one and return it to the school office. If you have any suggestions or comments, they would be greatly appreciated. You may use the back of this sheet for that purpose.

Thank you very much!

INSTRUCTIONS FOR OBSERVERS

Materials included in kit:

1. Folders and crayons for making identification cards. If more of these are needed, please let us know.

2. Catalogs of mental health publications. These are free. We want to encourage groups to write or come to the Austin-Travis County Society for Mental Health, 2410 San Antonio, to select booklets in which they are interested.

3. Six Observer's Tally Sheets, one for each meeting. Please fill out the top section and list the names of each person attending this meeting. This will be our attendance record. For each remark made during the discussion, make a small mark by the speaker's name in the column headed "Verbalization." In addition, if the remark made is of a personal nature or refers to a personal experience, make another mark in the column headed "Personal Reference."

4. Six stamped addressed envelopes for your convenience in mailing us the tally sheets after each meeting along with information about any new group members. Please mail these as soon as convenient after each meeting.

Please keep a careful check of attendance. You will have a list of names, addresses, and telephone numbers of all those who have registered for your group. It is important for us to have this information about each new person who comes into the group, as well as a complete attendance record for each meeting.

Individual arrangements will be made about the whereabouts of the film, projector, etc. Please replace film in its box, not rewound, and fill out the card that is with it.

APPENDIX B

Miscellaneous Tables

TABLE B-1

Analysis of Variance for Research Categories, Using Initial Scores on the Parent-Attitude Survey
(796 Subjects)

Parent-Attitude Survey Scale	Source of Variation	Degrees of Freedom	Variance Estimate	F	*p*
Confidence	Between	9	37.7	0.64	..
	Within	786	57.4		
Causation	Between	9	83.3	1.48	..
	Within	786	56.1		
Acceptance	Between	9	163.8	2.13	.05
	Within	786	76.7		
Understanding	Between	9	35.3	0.79	..
	Within	786	44.7		
Trust	Between	9	133.2	1.84	..
	Within	786	72.3		

TABLE B-2

Analysis of Variance for Age of Child, Using Initial Scores on the Parent-Attitude Survey
(793 Subjects)

Parent-Attitude Survey Scale	Source of Variation	Degrees of Freedom	Variance Estimate	F	*p*
Confidence	Between	6	75.8	1.33	. .
	Within	786	57.0		
Causation	Between	6	272.3	5.04	.001
	Within	786	54.1		
Acceptance	Between	6	338.0	4.46	.001
	Within	786	75.8		
Understanding	Between	6	64.3	1.49	. .
	Within	786	43.2		
Trust	Between	6	248.5	3.47	.001
	Within	786	71.7		

TABLE B-3

Analysis of Variance for Type of School (Grouped by Socioeconomic Level), Sex of Child, and Sex of Parent, Using Initial Scores on the Parent-Attitude Survey
(162 Subjects)

Parent-Attitude Survey Scale	Source of Variation[1]	Degrees of Freedom	Variance Estimate	F	*p*
Confidence	School	2	260.4	5.80	.001
	Sex of child	1	23.6		
	Sex of parent	1	54.6	1.22	. .
	Within	142	44.9		
Causation	School	2	569.5	10.20	.001
	Sex of child	1	20.2		
	Sex of parent	1	260.6	4.67	.05
	Within	142	55.8		
Acceptance	School	2	793.1	15.20	.001
	Sex of child	1	55.6	1.06	
	Sex of parent	1	691.2	13.24	.001
	Within	142	52.2		
Understanding	School	2	401.8	8.53	.001
	Sex of child	1	21.0		
	Sex of parent	1	479.5	10.18	.01
	Within	142	47.1		
Trust	School	2	754.6	12.71	.001
	Sex of child	1	166.0	2.80	
	Sex of parent	1	1,044.2	17.59	.001
	Within	142	59.4		

[1] Of the many two-way interactions (not shown), only two were significant: School-by-Parent (on Causation) at the .01 level, and School-by-Parent (on Understanding) at the .05 level. None of the three-way interactions was significant.

TABLE B-4

Analysis of Variance for Type of School (Grouped by Socioeconomic Level), Research Category, and Sex, Using Initial Scores from the Sociometric Evaluation
(546 Subjects)

Source[1]	Degrees of Freedom	Variance Estimate	F	*p*
School	3	0.93	1.24	. .
Research category	2	0.39	0.52	. .
Sex	1	4.10	5.47	.05
Within	518	0.75		

[1] None of the interactions was significant and none is shown.

TABLE B-5

Analysis of Variance for Type of School (Grouped by Socioeconomic Level), Research Category, and Sex, Using Initial Ratings by Teachers
(546 Subjects)

Source[1]	Degrees of Freedom	Variance Estimate	F	*p*
School	3	0.92	0.22	. .
Research category	2	0.69	0.17	. .
Sex	1	38.47	9.25	.01
Within	518	4.16		

[1] None of the interactions was significant and none is shown.

TABLE B-6

Variables for Factor Analysis

[1]1.	School district, grouped by socioeconomic level	
[1]2.	Research category	
3.	Sex of child	
4.	Age of child	
5.	Grade of child	
6.	Initial sociometric standard score of child	
[1]7.	Initial teacher rating of child	
8.	Confidence	Initial Parent-Attitude Survey
9.	Causation	Initial Parent-Attitude Survey
10.	Acceptance	Initial Parent-Attitude Survey
11.	Understanding	Initial Parent-Attitude Survey
12.	Trust	Initial Parent-Attitude Survey
13.	Deviant-response scale	
14.	Religious affiliation	
15.	Density of traffic in neighborhood	
16.	Spacing of dwelling units in neighborhood	
[1]17.	Play space for children in neighborhood	
[1]18.	Condition of neighborhood	
19.	Amount of living space in the home	
[1]20.	Condition of the home	
[1]21.	Comparison of home with others in neighborhood	
22.	Number of children in family	
23.	Mother's age	
24.	Mother's education	
25.	Mother's occupation	
26.	Father's age	
27.	Father's education	
28.	Father's occupation	
[1]29.	Frequency of church attendance	
[2]30.	Final minus initial sociometric standard score of child	
[1]31.	Final minus initial teacher rating of child	
32.	Confidence	Final Minus Initial Parent-Attitude Survey
33.	Causation	Final Minus Initial Parent-Attitude Survey
34.	Acceptance	Final Minus Initial Parent-Attitude Survey
35.	Understanding	Final Minus Initial Parent-Attitude Survey
36.	Trust	Final Minus Initial Parent-Attitude Survey

[1] Direction of these variables reversed from original measurement.

[2] Variables 30–36 are difference scores rather than initial measurements, obtained by subtracting the initial score from the final score. These difference scores were included in the factor analysis because at one time their use as a measurement of change was considered. Since a more appropriate method (analysis of covariance) was available, the difference scores were not used and appear nowhere else in the study.

TABLE B-7

Intercorrelations of 36 Variables for 613 Cases

Variable No.	Variable No. *2	3	4	5	6	*7	8	9	10	11	12	13	14	15	16
* 1	**	**	–15	–08	**	**	28	35	44	33	35	–15	**	09	16
* 2		**	–13	–13	–08	**	–08	**	11	**	07	**	07	13	**
3			**	**	–07	–11	**	**	**	**	**	**	**	**	07
4				94	**	**	–11	–16	–16	**	–16	**	**	–07	**
5					**	**	–08	–11	–12	**	–11	**	**	–09	**
6						47	07	13	**	**	**	**	**	**	**
* 7							07	07	**	**	**	**	07	**	**
8								55	47	46	46	**	09	07	12
9									53	62	47	**	15	**	**
10										52	62	**	23	**	11
11											47	13	22	**	**
12												**	20	**	08
13													–10	**	**
14														**	**
15															09
16															
*17															
*18															
19															
*20															
*21															
22															
23															
24															
25															
26															
27															
28															
*29															
30															
*31															
32															
33															
34															
35															

* Direction of these variables is reversed from original measurements.

** Correlations less than .07 ($p = .05$) are not shown.

Variable No.

*17	*18	19	*20	*21	22	23	24	25	26	27	28	*29	30	*31	32	33	34	35	36
29	36	34	27	**	–22	**	43	**	**	39	38	**	**	**	**	**	–13	**	–11
**	**	**	13	**	–08	**	09	–16	**	13	**	**	08	10	**	**	**	**	**
**	**	**	**	–07	**	**	**	**	**	–10	**	**	**	**	**	**	**	**	**
**	**	**	–08	–07	18	29	–14	**	17	–19	–12	**	**	**	**	**	**	**	**
**	**	**	**	**	16	29	**	**	19	–12	**	**	**	**	**	**	**	**	**
–07	**	08	**	08	**	**	**	**	**	**	**	**	–45	**	**	**	**	**	**
**	09	13	10	09	**	**	**	**	**	14	**	**	**	–42	**	**	**	**	**
10	10	17	12	**	–17	**	31	07	**	25	25	**	**	**	–43	–07	–17	–11	–12
**	07	11	10	**	–20	–18	36	**	–11	30	26	**	**	**	–12	–36	–15	–21	–10
16	21	22	16	**	–13	–08	48	**	**	39	35	**	**	**	–07	**	–41	–10	–10
**	**	11	09	**	–13	**	38	**	**	27	25	**	**	**	**	–07	–10	–37	**
08	11	14	15	**	–18	**	43	**	**	36	29	**	**	**	**	**	–16	–08	–37
–07	–10	–14	–12	–10	09	**	–14	**	**	–14	–08	**	**	**	**	07	**	**	**
**	**	**	**	**	–14	**	32	**	**	21	10	**	**	**	**	**	**	**	**
19	07	19	11	**	**	**	**	–10	**	09	**	**	07	**	**	**	**	**	**
26	15	25	11	**	**	**	**	**	**	09	17	**	**	**	**	**	–08	**	–07
	30	22	25	**	**	07	18	–10	13	22	15	08	08	**	**	**	**	**	**
		43	50	09	–14	**	26	**	08	25	18	10	07	**	**	**	–09	**	**
			37	21	–23	**	27	**	**	26	21	**	**	–07	**	**	**	**	**
				39	–31	**	23	**	**	25	11	10	**	**	**	**	**	**	**
					–22	**	09	**	**	14	**	**	**	**	**	**	**	**	**
						14	–17	–10	14	–10	–09	**	**	**	**	**	**	**	**
							**	**	62	**	**	**	**	**	**	**	**	07	**
								14	**	62	44	10	**	**	**	**	–09	**	–09
									–12	**	**	**	**	–08	**	**	**	**	**
										13	16	07	11	**	**	**	**	**	**
											50	12	08	**	**	**	–09	**	**
												10	**	**	**	**	–11	**	**
													**	**	**	**	**	**	**
														11	**	07	**	**	**
															**	**	**	**	**
																34	24	22	23
																	33	36	28
																		24	30
																			23

TABLE B-8

Rotated Factor Loadings**

Variable Number	Factor Number I	II	III	IV	V	VI	VII	VIII	IX	X	XI	h²
* 1	37	–22					39			–29		47
* 2								37				19
3									25			08
4				94								94
5				93								91
6					–71							57
* 7					–33				–20		–57	50
8	59		21		–24		24					57
9	73								–25			71
10	73								26	–25		73
11	76								–35			73
12	68									–24		61
13		24										11
14	20									–29		18
15							29	24				17
16							44					21
*17							51					33
*18		–45					38				–20	46
19		–48					42	–21				45
*20		–69					21					59
*21		–45										24
22		44										28
23						–77						63
24	35	–20								–71		68
25								–39				17
26						–76						61
27	21									–70		64
28	23						23			–51		39
*29												05
30					52							30
*31											50	29
32			–53								–30	41
33			–60						26			47
34			–56									39
35			–50						41			44
36			–51									33

* Direction of these variables reversed from measurement.
** Factor loadings below .20 not shown.

TABLE B-9

Chi-Square Analysis of Frequency of Change of Response from Initial Interview to Final Interview by the Four Research Categories

Question No.	Question Content	Respondents	χ^2	p df = 3
1	Difficulties in raising children	844	1.24	..
1-*a*	Parental response to difficulties	849	8.86	.05
1-*b*	Effectiveness of parental response to difficulties	849	9.75	.05
1-*c*	Cause of difficulties	849	8.16	.05
1-*d*	Commonness of difficulty	844	5.03	..
1-*e*	Outside help for solving difficulty	849	7.89	.05
1-*f*	Effectiveness of outside help	421	4.78	..
2	What parents like about parenthood	849	9.59	.05
2-*a*	Parental effectiveness	843	1.02	..
2-*b*	How parents account for their effectiveness	847	1.26	..
3	Parental worries	846	8.20	.05
3-*b*	Parental ineffectiveness	847	1.85	..
4	Amount of freedom given child	849	1.35	..
4-*c*	Parental restrictions on playmates	849	1.47	..
5	Methods of punishment	849	8.39	.05
5-*b*	What parents punish for	849	8.65	.05
5-*c*	Effectiveness of punishment	849	9.03	.05
6	Cause of family troubles	849	7.15	..
6-*a*	Who is involved in family troubles	849	4.23	..
6-*c*	Outsiders taking care of children	849	8.09	.05
6-*d*	Whether outsiders cause trouble	188	8.66	.05
7	Characteristics of the ideal child	845	2.94	..
7-*d*	Characteristics of the ideal parent	848	2.99	..

TABLE B-10

Chi-Square Analysis of Frequency of Change of Response from Initial Interview to Final Interview within the Discussion Group by Number of Meetings Attended

Question No.	Question Content	Respondents	χ^2	p df = 3
1	Difficulties in raising children	284	1.76	..
1-*a*	Parental response to difficulties	284	6.05	.05
1-*b*	Effectiveness of parental response to difficulties	284	5.02	..
1-*c*	Cause of difficulties	284	2.25	..
1-*d*	Commonness of difficulty	284	4.67	..
1-*e*	Outside help for solving difficulty	284	6.76	.05
1-*f*	Effectiveness of outside help	77	2.97	..
2	What parents like about parenthood	284	1.03	..
2-*a*	Parental effectiveness	284	2.21	..
2-*b*	How parents account for their effectiveness	284	2.94	..
3	Parental worries	284	1.76	..
3-*b*	Parental ineffectiveness	284	0.25	..
4	Amount of freedom given child	284	3.14	..
4-*c*	Parental restrictions on playmates	284	2.07	..
5	Methods of punishment	284	2.84	..
5-*b*	What parents punish for	284	3.84	..
5-*c*	Effectiveness of punishment	284	4.06	..
6	Cause of family troubles	284	5.61	..
6-*a*	Who is involved in family troubles	284	1.64	..
6-*c*	Outsiders taking care of children	284	3.72	..
6-*d*	Whether outsiders cause trouble	64	2.94	..
7	Characteristics of the ideal child	284	2.13	..
7-*d*	Characteristics of the ideal parent	284	2.71	..

TABLE B-11

Chi-Square Analysis of Frequency of Change of Response from Initial Interview to Final Interview within the Discussion Group by Frequency of Verbal Participation

Question No.	Question Content	Respondents	χ^2	p df = 3
1	Difficulties in raising children	284	2.01	. .
1-*a*	Parental response to difficulties	284	2.88	. .
1-*b*	Effectiveness of parental response to difficulties	284	2.63	. .
1-*c*	Cause of difficulties	284	9.62	.05
1-*d*	Commonness of difficulty	284	5.04	. .
1-*e*	Outside help for solving difficulty	284	0.88	. .
1-*f*	Effectiveness of outside help	77	1.02	. .
2	What parents like about parenthood	284	6.53	. .
2-*a*	Parental effectiveness	284	2.33	. .
2-*b*	How parents account for their effectiveness	284	3.57	. .
3	Parental worries	284	2.07	. .
3-*b*	Parental ineffectiveness	284	2.52	. .
4	Amount of freedom given child	284	4.61	. .
4-*c*	Parental restrictions on playmates	284	1.62	. .
5	Methods of punishment	284	2.82	. .
5-*b*	What parents punish for	284	4.91	. .
5-*c*	Effectiveness of punishment	284	5.83	. .
6	Cause of family troubles	284	3.90	. .
6-*a*	Who is involved in family troubles	284	0.78	. .
6-*c*	Outsiders taking care of children	284	6.48	. .
6-*d*	Whether outsiders cause trouble	64	6.94	. .
7	Characteristics of the ideal child	284	3.01	. .
7-*d*	Characteristics of the ideal parent	284	2.46	. .

TABLE B-12

Chi-Square Analysis of Frequency of Change of Response from Initial Interview to Final Interview within the Discussion Group by Percentage of Personal References

Question No.	Question Content	Respondents	χ^2	p df = 3
1	Difficulties in raising children	284	1.68	. .
1-*a*	Parental response to difficulties	284	1.74	. .
1-*b*	Effectiveness of parental responses to difficulties	284	2.83	. .
1-*c*	Cause of difficulties	284	8.58	.05
1-*d*	Commonness of difficulty	284	1.34	. .
1-*e*	Outside help	284	2.82	. .
1-*f*	Effectiveness of outside help	77	2.16	. .
2	What parents like about parenthood	284	1.80	. .
2-*a*	Parental effectiveness	284	0.05	. .
2-*b*	How parents account for their effectiveness	284	8.33	.05
3	Parental worries	284	0.98	. .
3-*b*	Parental ineffectiveness	284	3.64	. .
4	Amount of freedom given child	284	1.02	. .
4-*c*	Parental restrictions on playmates	284	1.49	. .
5	Methods of punishment	284	2.45	. .
5-*b*	What parents punish for	284	4.78	. .
5-*c*	Effectiveness of punishment	284	6.03	. .
6	Cause of family troubles	284	1.88	. .
6-*a*	Who is involved in family troubles	284	1.12	. .
6-*c*	Outsiders taking care of children	284	5.97	. .
6-*d*	Do outsiders cause trouble	64	6.79	. .
7	Characteristics of the ideal child	284	4.68	. .
7-*d*	Characteristics of the ideal parent	284	3.71	. .

APPENDIX C

Films and Plays Used in Group Discussions

Number of Times Shown	*Title, Description, and Source*
23	*From Sociable Six to Noisy Nine* (21 minutes, sound, black and white), produced by the National Film Board of Canada, distributed by McGraw-Hill Book Co., Tcxt-Film Department, 330 Wesl 42nd Street, New York 36, N.Y.
22	*Preface to a Life* (29 minutes, sound, black and white), produced by Sun Dial Films, Inc., for the National Institute of Mental Health in 1950, distributed by United World Films, 1445 Park Avenue, New York 29, N.Y.
15	*Children's Emotions* (22 minutes, sound, black and white), produced by Crawley Films, Ltd., in 1950, distributed by McGraw-Hill Book Co., Text-Film Department, 330 West 42nd Street, New York 36, New York.
15	*Shyness* (23 minutes, sound, black and white), produced by the National Film Board of Canada in 1953, distributed by McGraw-Hill Book Co., Text-Film Department, 330 West 42nd Street, New York 36, N.Y.
13	*Fears of Children* (32 minutes, sound, black and white), produced by Julian Bryan, International Film Foundation, for the Oklahoma Mental Health Authority and the Mental Health Film Board, Inc., in 1952, distributed by International Film Bureau, Inc., 57 East Jackson Boulevard, Chicago 4, Ill.
10	*Parents Are People, Too* (15 minutes, sound, black and white), produced by McGraw-Hill Text Films in 1955, distributed by McGraw-Hill Book Co., Text-Film Department, 330 West 42nd Street, New York 36, N.Y.
9	*Anger At Work* (21 minutes, sound, black and white), produced by the University of Oklahoma under the sponsorship of the Oklahoma State Department of Health, distributed by International Film Bureau, Inc., 57 East Jackson Boulevard, Chicago 4, Ill.
7	*From Ten to Twelve* (26 minutes, sound, black and white), produced by the National Film Board of Canada in 1957, distributed by McGraw-Hill Book Co., Text-Film Department, 330 West 42nd Street, New York 36, N.Y.
6	*Families First* (17 minutes, sound, black and white), produced by RKO-Pathé for the New York State Youth Commission in 1948, distributed by the New York State Youth Commission, 66 Beaver Street, Albany 7, N.Y.
6	*Meeting Emotional Needs in Childhood* (33 minutes, sound, black and white), produced by the Department of Child Study, Vassar College, in 1947, distributed by New York University Film Library, 26 Washington Place, New York 3, N.Y.

Number of Times Shown	*Title, Description, and Source*
5	*Development of Individual Differences* (13 minutes, sound, black and white), produced by McGraw-Hill Text Films in 1957, distributed by McGraw-Hill Book Co., Text-Film Department, 330 West 42nd Street, New York 36, N.Y.
5	*He Acts His Age* (14 minutes, sound, black and white), produced by Crawley Films, Ltd., in 1949, distributed by McGraw-Hill Book Co., Text-Film Department, 330 West 42nd Street, New York 36, N.Y.
3	*The Family* (20 minutes, sound, black and white), produced by the U.S. Army in 1952, distributed by United World Films, Inc., 1445 Park Avenue, New York 29, N.Y.
3	*Social Development* (16 minutes, sound, black and white), produced by Crawley Films, Ltd., in 1950, distributed by McGraw-Hill Book Co., Text-Film Department, 330 West 42nd Street, New York 36, New York.
3	*Sibling Rivalries and Parents* (11 minutes, sound, black and white), produced by Crawley Films, Ltd., in 1956, distributed by McGraw-Hill Book Co., Text-Film Department, 330 West 42nd Street, New York 36, N.Y.
2	*Farewell to Childhood* (20 minutes, sound, black and white), produced by Herbert Kerkow, Inc., for the North Carolina Mental Health Authority and the Mental Health Film Board, Inc., in 1952, distributed by International Film Bureau, Inc., 57 East Jackson Boulevard, Chicago 4, Ill.
2	*Human Growth* (19 minutes, sound, color), produced by the E. C. Brown Trust in cooperation with the University of Oregon in 1948, distributed by the E. C. Brown Trust, 220 S.W. Alder Street, Portland 4, Oregon.
2	*Age of Turmoil* (20 minutes, sound, black and white), produced by Crawley Films, Ltd., distributed by McGraw-Hill Book Co., Text-Film Department, 330 West 42nd Street, New York 36, N.Y.
2	*Learning to Understand Children* (22 minutes, sound, black and white), produced by McGraw-Hill Text Films in 1947, distributed by McGraw-Hill Book Co., Text-Film Department, 330 West 42nd Street, New York 36, N.Y.
2	*Meeting the Needs of Adolescents* (19 minutes, sound, black and white), produced by Crawley Films for the National Film Board of Canada in 1953, distributed by McGraw-Hill Book Co., Text-Film Department, 330 West 42nd Street, New York 36, N.Y.
2	*Developmental Characteristics of Preadolescents* (18 minutes, sound, black and white), produced by McGraw-Hill Text Films in 1954, distributed by McGraw-Hill Book Co., Text-Film Department, 330 West 42nd Street, New York 36, N.Y.

Number of Times Shown	*Title, Description, and Source*
2	*The Importance of Goals* (19 minutes, sound, black and white), produced by Audio Productions, Inc., in 1951, distributed by McGraw-Hill Book Co., Text-Film Department, 330 West 42nd Street, New York 36, N.Y.
1	*The Frustrating Fours and Fascinating Fives* (22 minutes, sound, black and white), produced by the National Film Board of Canada in 1952, distributed by McGraw-Hill Book Co., Text-Film Department, 330 West 42nd Street, New York 36, N.Y.
1	*Human Beginnings* (22 minutes, sound, color), produced by Eddie Albert Productions in cooperation with Dr. Lester Beck of the University of Oregon in 1950, distributed by Association Films, Inc., 347 Madison Avenue, New York 17, N.Y.
1	*The High Wall* (30 minutes, sound, black and white), produced jointly by the Columbia Foundation of San Francisco, State of Illinois Departments of Public Instruction and Welfare, and the Anti-Defamation League of B'nai B'rith in 1952, distributed by McGraw-Hill Book Co., Text-Film Department, 330 West 42nd Street, New York 36, N.Y.
1	*The Teens* (26 minutes, sound, black and white), produced by the National Film Board of Canada in 1958, distributed by McGraw-Hill Book Co., Text-Film Department, 330 West 42nd Street, New York 36, N.Y.
1	*A Place to Live* (26 minutes, sound, black and white), produced for the National Social Welfare Assembly by Dynamic Films, Inc., in 1955, distributed by Dynamic Films, Inc., 405 Park Avenue, New York 22, N.Y.
1	*According to Size,* distributed by the National Association for Mental Health, 10 Columbus Circle, New York 19, N.Y.
1	*The Case of the Missing Handshake,* distributed by the National Association for Mental Health, 10 Columbus Circle, New York 19, N.Y.
1	*The Will B. Mature Family,* distributed by the National Association for Mental Health, 10 Columbus Circle, New York 19, N.Y.

APPENDIX D

Project Personnel

STAFF

Research Director		
	Carl F. Hereford, Ph.D.	1955–1960
Director of Community Education		
	Frank Cheavens, Ph.D.	1956–1957
	Len Jordan, M.A.	1957–1958
	Mrs. Jack C. Eisenberg	1958–1960
Research Assistant (half-time)		
	James G. Kelly, Ph.D.	1956–1957
	John McBrearty, Ph.D.	1956–1957
	Paul B. Rothaus, Ph.D.	1957–1958
	Edward Moseley, Ph.D.	1958–1960
Secretary		
	Mrs. James Eichelberger	1955–1958
	Mrs. Charles Cleland	1958–1959
	Mrs. Elmer Huber	1959–1960
	Mrs. W. W. Hunt (part-time)	1956–1960

RESEARCH COUNCIL

[1,2]William C. Adamson, M.D.	[3]Austin Community Guidance Center
[2]John A. Boston, Jr., M.D.	Austin Community Guidance Center
[1]Ernestine Bowen, Ed.D.	[3]Texas State Department of Health
[1]Oliver H. Bown, Ph.D.	University of Texas
Bert D. Burnes, M.A.	Austin Public Schools
[1]Irby Carruth	Austin Public Schools
[1,2]Charles H. Dent, Ed.D.	University of Texas
[1]Wayne H. Holtzman, Ph.D.	Hogg Foundation for Mental Health
[1]Ruth Huey, M.S.	Texas Education Agency
[1]Ira Iscoe, Ph.D.	University of Texas
Wallace Mandell, Ph.D.	[3]Texas State Department of Health
[1]Carson McGuire, Ph.D.	University of Texas
[1]Charles Mitchell, M.S.W.	Texas State Department of Health
[1]Bernice Moore, Ph.D.	Hogg Foundation for Mental Health
[1]Harry Moore, Ph.D.	University of Texas
John Pierce-Jones, Ph.D.	University of Texas
Glenn V. Ramsey, Ed.D.	Austin, Texas
[1]DeWitt Reddick, Ph.D.	University of Texas
[1]Dwight Rieman, M.S.W.	Texas State Department of Health
[1]Sylvia Sonder, Ph.D.	[3]Austin State Hospital
[1]Philip Worchel, Ph.D.	University of Texas

[1] Member of the original Research Council.
[2] Co-investigator.
[3] No longer at this institution.

Index